IMPROVING YOUR STAND UP PADDLEBOARDING

IMPROVING YOUR STAND UP PADDLEBOARDING

**A guide to getting the most out of your SUP:
Touring, racing, yoga & surf**

Andy Burrows & James van Drunen

FERNHURST
BOOKS

Published in 2022 by Fernhurst Books Limited
© 2022 Fernhurst Books Limited

The Windmill, Mill Lane, Harbury, Leamington
Spa, Warwickshire. CV33 9HP, UK
Tel: +44 (0) 1926 337488 | www.fernhurstbooks.
com

A catalogue record for this book is available from
the British Library
ISBN 978-1-912621-43-9

Designed by Daniel Stephen
Printed in India by Replika Press

CONTENTS

INTRODUCTION 6

UNDERSTANDING HOW TO IMPROVE 8

IMPROVE YOUR EFFICIENCY 22

IMPROVE YOUR TECHNIQUE...39

IMPROVE YOUR SKILLS 58

IMPROVE YOUR PHYSICAL CAPABILITY...........................80

PARTICIPATING...106

BEING PROPERLY EQUIPPED...128

THE FLOW STATE, MASTERY & HAPPINESS...................149

INTRODUCTION

Stand Up Paddleboarding is special. Many elements of the activity make it attractive to people of all physical abilities. Being able to stand on the water creates a very different viewpoint from sitting. Furthermore, most people can progress to standing on a board and paddling within minutes.

SUP offers a higher degree of freedom when compared to most watersports. With equipment that is easily transportable, it is simple to organise and embark on a trip. The paddle affords propulsion in any direction and can be used successfully in calm or challenging conditions. It's an activity where you can go out on any day and not be beholden to the weather or the wind.

SUP has opened up access to the water for thousands who never entertained canoeing, windsurfing or surfing. During the 2020 lockdowns, SUP inflatable sales were such that suppliers across the UK and Europe ran out of stock.

Now participation in SUP clubs and groups is building across Europe. People who started out on a 'try it and see' basis are becoming SUP addicts. They enjoy the blend of physical, spiritual and social experiences.

SUP offers incredible variety. Calm and flat, to wind, waves or flowing river: there is always something to challenge yourself and learn from. Go out for a run, and your mind can wander, and your legs will take you automatically where you want to go. This is a time to switch off and relax. Go out on the board, and your mind becomes sharpened as it examines the dynamics in front of it. Which way is the wind blowing, where is the swell, are my hands vertical? Paddling is like a mantra taking you towards a meditative state. The mind cannot wander; instead, it intensifies in the moment. In a world where most of us suffer from the inability to focus for longer than a few minutes, SUP can demand total attention.

The growing popularity of SUP is being reflected in more dedicated participation in organised events. The SUP race calendar continues to grow across Europe. But it is noticeable how many people enjoy going out in social groups. To feel the spirit of adventure with others provides excitement and confidence at the same time.

Meanwhile, there is a growing group of adrenaline junkies hopping on waves or flying down white water rapids. SUP yoga has offered a fresh and different challenge to the land-based practice and has consequently generated a large following. In short, SUP appeals to a vast body of people of different ages and interests.

We wrote this book to share our thoughts on how anyone can get better at SUP. Many books have already been written covering the basics of the stroke to help those starting out. We wanted to help people who can already SUP to do it better. We wanted to inspire them with the desire to continuously improve, experiment and enjoy.

Humans are happiest when striving. An easy win is not as satisfying as a hard-worked-for reward. It's part of the human condition.

Our proposition is that happiness is found in taking part in the journey to be better. It's not the destination that will make you happy.

SUP has been fantastic for us in different ways. For James, SUP literally changed his life. As a young teenager, he was overweight and bullied. His first experience on a SUP saw him easily 'beaten' by his sister. This ignited something in him and, within two years, he was one of the top three paddlers in Spain. Since then, he has completed the 11 Cities (a 220km race in The Netherlands) on four occasions, won podium positions on the Eurotour (a series of Europe's biggest SUP races) and is now a highly recognised SUP coach, operating his own business out of Javea on the Costa Blanca in Spain.

For Andy, a person in his late fifties, SUP has been a journey of technical learning and broader life lessons. As a result, he has become fitter, stronger and more resilient. He was lucky to meet James at his first race in Javea three years ago. Andy was on a 10-foot inflatable, and James was on his 14-foot race board in seas with a 3m swell. James won that day and covered 10km in half the time it took Andy to do 5km on his knees. Since that day, he has come a long way on a SUP board, and even recently competed in the SUP World Festival. But he recognises that he still has much to learn!

These days we often go out and enjoy training together. We have very different lessons to learn, but SUP brings us together as an activity, a sport and a compelling common interest.

We hope our love and enthusiasm for SUP radiates through this book. Whatever your interest and ability, we hope you enjoy its content and find some useful ideas and tips to inspire you on your SUP journey.

James and Andy training together in Javea

CHAPTER 1

UNDER-STANDING HOW TO IMPROVE

THE JOURNEY TO UNCONSCIOUS COMPETENCE

SUP involves an interplay between your mind, body and the environment. You take a particular action and receive immediate feedback. For example, if you put your weight on one side of the board, you instantly feel it move to that side. Try a particular paddle stroke and you will feel the board respond in a certain way. Adopt a different stance, and your body will feel new sensations of balance. Sometimes the feedback is inconsequential and at others it is highly rewarding, such as when you perform the actions to catch a breaking wave successfully.

You find yourself involved in a continuous loop, where an action causes a reaction which necessitates a further action. If you consider the true extent of the complexity of what is involved in just standing on a paddleboard, you might wonder how it is even possible. Sensory inputs are being processed at a rate of thousands per second. Your body makes instant corrections before conscious thought has time to get involved. If conscious thought

did interfere, you would soon be in the water!

Watch a pro and much of what they do is down to what is known as 'unconscious competence'. They exhibit incredible skill without conscious thought. They look natural and have complete trust in their abilities.

They were not always like this. They developed knowledge, skill and confidence over time. Thousands of hours on the water in all kinds of conditions and situations. Becoming adept on the water takes a long time – even for the elite.

Many newcomers to SUP have entered the activity later in their years. Their rate of skill acquisition is inevitably slower than a young person brought up on the water. The prospect of hitting pro performance if you start SUP after the age of 40 is slim. But incredible progress can still be made, and with it comes deep satisfaction. Chess has been said to be an activity that takes 10 minutes to learn and a lifetime to master. SUP is the physical equivalent.

James, a professional paddler

Comfort zones are places stored in the mind where the paddler can undertake something automatically without conscious thought. Comfort zones are pleasant areas to operate in because they can calm the mind and provide an opportunity to 'defragment'. The ability to do something while thinking about something else can be therapeutic. This is what occurs when going for a walk in nature. A SUP tour along a rocky coastline on flat turquoise seas can have a similar effect. But paddle in your comfort zone all the time, and you will not improve as a paddler. In fact, you will go backwards.

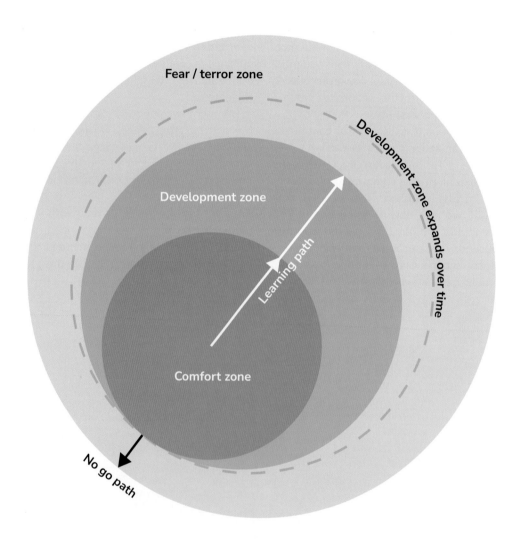

Expanding the comfort zone
For example: learning to catch waves that are intimidating: don't even go there to start with; learn skills to enable you to push / build the development zone into the 'fear zone'

Unlike walking, paddling is not 'natural'. It is necessarily convoluted because you have to adopt a series of complex positions to successfully move the board on the water. Consequently, paddling is much more prone to error than walking or cycling. There are many more variables to consider.

The act of paddling needs to be deliberate and thought about. To achieve unconscious competence, we need to first be consciously competent.

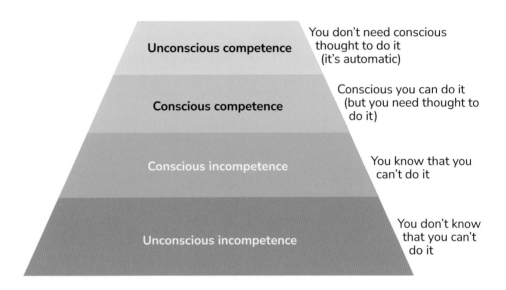

Unconscious competence — You don't need conscious thought to do it (it's automatic)

Conscious competence — Conscious you can do it (but you need thought to do it)

Conscious incompetence — You know that you can't do it

Unconscious incompetence — You don't know that you can't do it

The ladder to unconscious competence and higher performance

A 'good' paddle stroke is an act of precision. You can feel a distinct difference between a good and a bad stroke. And because you might be doing 3,000 strokes in a session, there is a vast difference in the result of 3,000 good strokes versus 3,000 bad ones.

The pathway to improvement is a long and windy one. This is why SUP is addictive – because it is not easy to do well and offers many rewards along the way.

THE ABILITY TO 'FEEL' IS THE STARTING POINT FOR IMPROVEMENT

Someone highly skilled has 'feel'. This feel translates into intuition. They can tune into the many sensory inputs and make sense of them without thinking. This sensation has been described as 'flow', and Chapter 8 looks at this in more detail. Feelings of flow are closely associated with feelings of happiness. Flow can only be sourced by a deep and continuing desire to improve at something.

Awareness develops intuition. The paddler should always have these three areas in mind:

- What is going on in your **body** – the muscles you are using, how you are breathing, your stance, your balance, your feet and the level of tension in your body
- What is going on in your **mind** – the emotions: are you feeling happy, sad, confident, fearful, tired, energised?
- What is happening **around you** – awareness of the wind, the sea and other people

A paddler needs to be aware of what is going on in their body, their mind and around them

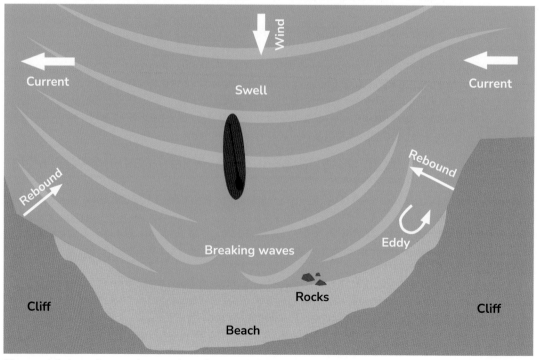

The paddleboarder can have a lot of natural dynamics to contend with

ROUTES TO LEARNING

Self-learning: People with an incentive to improve will constantly learn through personal experience. They can do this through many modalities, including books, magazine articles and videos. Information on its own does not translate into learning. Information provides awareness. But awareness without action cannot lead to learning. Self-learners constantly ask questions of themselves and others. They try new things and reflect on the results of their efforts.

Coaching: Having a coach provides an excellent opportunity to improve your paddling. A coach will have knowledge that they can share with you and, most importantly, they will provide feedback on your performance. (After all, it is not easy for paddlers to observe their own performance.)

A coach can provide encouragement, challenge and build confidence. These are all essential ingredients for anyone looking to take their paddling further.

A good coach will balance their knowledge and beliefs with their client's capability. There is little point in asking someone to do something that they are not physically capable of doing.

A coach can really help you improve your paddling

The Learning Cycle

Learning is stimulated by awareness and is achieved by completing these 5 phases:

PHASE 1:	PHASE 2:	PHASE 3:	PHASE 4:	PHASE 5:
We experience something	We reflect on the experience	We connect the experience with other experiences	We decide to do something different	We act in accordance with our decision to create a new experience
"I fell off near the rocks in the rebound while the others got away"	*"Why was I the only one to fall off?"*	*"It's not the first time that this has happened; the others always accelerate at that point while I slow down"*	*"The next time I enter that area, I will purposely accelerate and see if I can catch the rebounds"*	

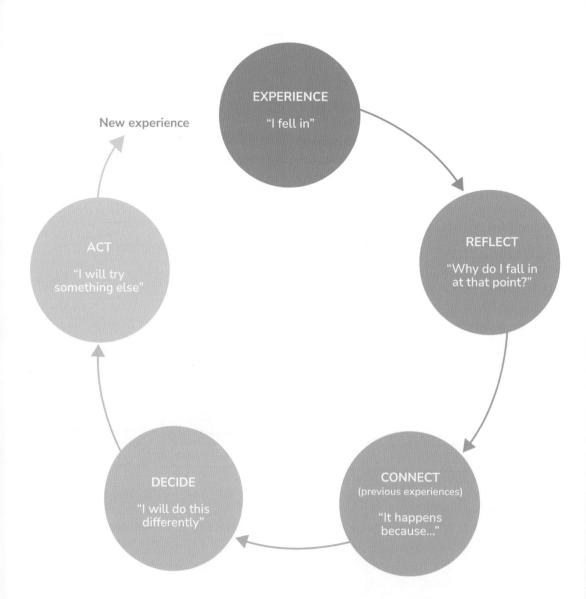

The learning cycle

In this example, the paddler tries the solution devised in phase 4 and then enters a new learning cycle. If the action is successful, they have learnt to deal with the problem area. If they didn't quite make it but felt there was an improvement, they could refine their approach. If the outcome was exactly the same as before, perhaps they need to adopt alternative actions.

This cycle is sometimes described as 'failing forwards'. Failing is not a particularly positive word, but the point here is that taking action after failure promotes learning.

Learning Environments

The situation and frame of mind both influence how you learn. The two extremes are:

1. A relaxed, controlled environment: When you make adjustments in easy conditions, learning is a controlled process. You remain within the boundaries of your comfort zone. In this zone, you are operating with certainty that your ability is more than sufficient to match the challenge. Undertaking drills where you break the stroke down into elements and practise isolated areas fall into this category. You are trying to train the body through repetition. Such repetition must always be mindful because it has no effect if it becomes mindless.

Experimenting in a controlled environment is an enjoyable way of learning. It is essential to improve complex challenges such as a step back turn. It makes perfect sense to start on flat water and perfect a series of moves before moving on to more complicated conditions. In fact, it would probably be counter-productive to try to learn a step back turn in a 15-knot wind and breaking waves. You might find yourself failing more than succeeding. This is not a good learning environment because you start to make failure a habit. You might get frustrated and end your session feeling that you don't want to try that again!

But learning also requires a degree of stress. Stress provides the mind with an incentive. So practising a step back turn on an icy loch might offer additional spice to the learning! You feel that you can do it, but know that you don't want to fall into the loch at 5°C. Achieving a clean turn in such circumstances somehow produces a greater sense of satisfaction than doing the exact same turn in the warmth of the Med in the middle of the summer!

Learning in a controlled environment: essential to improve complex challenges

2. Uncontrolled environment: Sometimes learning moves beyond the controlled environment. It's where you might feel you are no longer in complete control. It's a place where you are on the edge of your capability. These can be quite uncomfortable experiences at the time. However, when completed, they become transformational. Fear is a barrier to learning, and there is a delicate pivot point between fear and excitement.

Find yourself on a downwind: you are enjoying the wind on your back and you are rhythmically catching the waves. Then the wind suddenly gets up, the waves change and your whole feeling morphs into discomfort. These are times when you learn something about paddling and about yourself. At the time they can feel a bit surreal, but afterwards they can remind you how good it feels to be alive.

We are not advocating being reckless. But if you want to learn, you need to have some courage and take measured risks. What can really help here is sharing the experience with others. Whether it's adopting a tough pose on the SUP yoga board, tackling whitewater or going out with others on a windy day, challenging yourself is a great way to make progress. Success will make you feel more confident and more inclined to try things the next time.

Learning something in a less controlled environment can be uncomfortable, but it can also be transformational

IMPROVEMENT IS NEVER LINEAR

SUP is very rewarding to a newcomer. Most people progress from kneeling to standing to paddling within a relatively short time. Some people will assume that SUP is 'easy' because of this speed of achievement. But the chances are that they are at a stage where they think they are better than they are. The majority of paddlers that end up in difficulty, often swept out to sea by an offshore wind, are the ones with delusions of competence.

Improving at SUP is a stuttering, uneven process. You can make rapid progress followed by periods where you feel you are not improving at all. A paddler needs something to gauge progress against to have a sense of improvement. That comparator is usually another person. So if you always paddle solo, you may be in blissful ignorance of your true capabilities (or lack of them).

Paddling with another person allows you to gauge progress

Improvement is so fuzzy because our bodies and minds take time to adapt and internalise new things. Once internalisation has occurred, a sudden quantum leap is experienced. Such occasions can be the ability to catch water properly. You might have been practising for months. But one day, your body and mind are ready for it, and you feel a proper catch for the first time.

In a similar vein, catching waves can become a frustrating pursuit. You watch videos, you soldier out in the swell, but come back cold and empty-handed each time. Then one day, probably when you least expect it, something clicks, and you do it: you are riding your first wave.

The lessons here are:

1. Be patient. Good things come to those that wait.
2. Keep doing things correctly. There is no shortcut to success. You need to do the basics properly to progress.
3. Manage your activity to be in a zone between challenge and comfort. Don't set yourself up to fail, but continue to push yourself.
4. Accept that improvement is uneven.
5. Find someone to gauge yourself against.

GOALS CAN HELP DRIVE PERFORMANCE

Much has been written about the power of goals in directing performance. This is seen in the worlds of sport and business alike. Goals can be double-edged swords. They can motivate, and they can undermine. Goals that are not achieved can promote strong feelings of failure. Failure is generally not an emotion humans enjoy, and it might detract someone from doing SUP altogether.

Goals come in many forms. The acronym 'SMART' is often used to define a goal:

S Specific: well defined and easy to understand

M Measurable: a method of measuring the goal to see how close you are to achieving it

A Achievable

R Realistic: you have to believe it can be done in the timescale you have allocated to it

T Timebound: there is a timescale put on achieving the goal

Examples might be:
My goal is... *'To paddle down the River Tay from Pitlochry to Perth within the next 6 months.'*
My goal is... *'To paddle 1km in less than 6 minutes by 1 April 2023.'*

Goals may vary in timescale, such as 'I want to be world champion in ten years' vs 'I want to do 10km today.'

Goals might be a subset of a bigger goal.

Should you set goals? Research says they make a difference. Most sports people are driven and will naturally set goals. Other people reading this book for non-competitive reasons may not feel the need. Goal setting has a part to play in building conscious competence. The human mind is goal seeking and goal achieving. Even if you are not competitive, then setting goals will create energy.

Find the best goals for you. Goals that are 'outcome' focussed promote more pressure and the chance of failure than 'process' focussed ones:

- Outcome: 'I will be world champion in 2023'
- Process: 'I will train to compete in the world championships in 2023'

Identifying Areas To Focus On

The first stage of setting goals is to identify the areas you need to focus on. A useful way of doing this is to create a dartboard of the different aspects of your SUPing. These will be different for everyone, but we have included some examples below.

Filling out a dartboard is very simple. You start from the middle and colour one or more sections depending on how comfortable you feel with that skill: 1 = very low skill and 10 would be perfect. It is less about how you choose to rate yourself (which often shows more your confidence rather than your competence) and more about the differences in how you rate yourself in the individual areas.

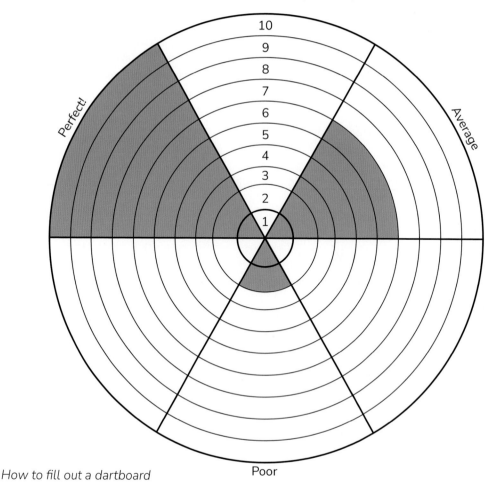

How to fill out a dartboard

The dartboard then shows you clearly the areas you need to work on which might be suitable for setting goals.

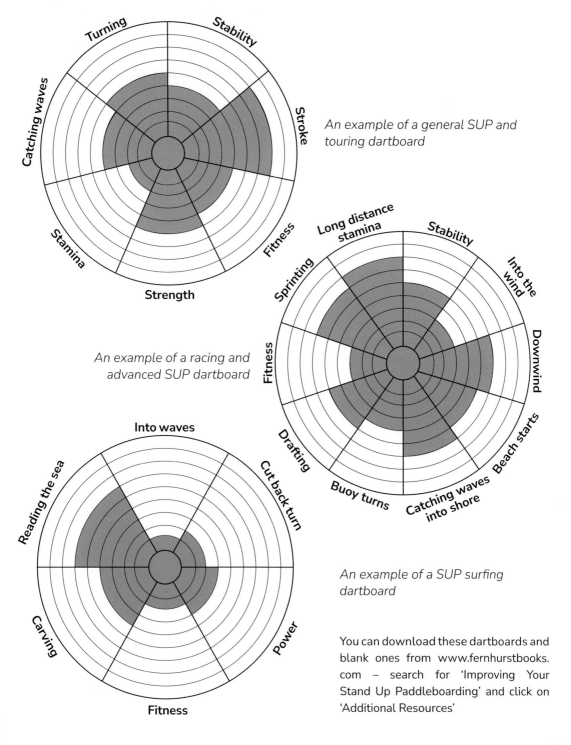

An example of a general SUP and touring dartboard

An example of a racing and advanced SUP dartboard

An example of a SUP surfing dartboard

You can download these dartboards and blank ones from www.fernhurstbooks. com – search for 'Improving Your Stand Up Paddleboarding' and click on 'Additional Resources'

Creating Goals In These Areas

Once you have identified the areas you need to work on, the GROW coaching model is a great process that you can use to identify personal goals that work for you, using a simple set of open questions. It is used in the profession of coaching as a process designed to elicit awareness and responsibility in the coachee.

GROW is a mnemonic:

G The Goal: a well-defined intention

R The Reality: what is taking place at present

O The Options: what actions could be taken

W The Will: the action to be taken

An example of how the coaching questions can be used (Q = question, R = reply):

Q. 'What is your goal in SUP?' (Goal)
R. 'To race in the elite category and be no more than 10 minutes behind the winner in a 10km race.'

Q. 'When would you like to achieve this goal?' (Goal)
R. 'Within 3 years.'

Q. 'So, where are you now?' (Reality)
R. 'I finish about 30 minutes behind in a 10km race.'

Q. 'What would be a realistic goal be for this season?' (Goal for this season)
R. 'To finish within 20 minutes of winners: to increase my speed over a 10km race by 10 minutes.'

Q. 'What happens in races at the moment?' (Reality)
R. 'I start well, but I run out of steam at the halfway mark and lose places.'

Q. 'What options do you have to change this?' (Options)
R. 'Buy a faster board, improve my stroke, buy a new paddle or get fitter!'

Q. 'Weigh up each option in terms of cost, ease and likely effect. Which option will you choose?' (Refining options)
R. 'Fitness.'

Q. 'How do you rate your fitness on a scale of 1 to 10 at the moment? 10 being excellent.' (Reality)
R. '6.'

Q. 'What does it need to be to achieve your goal?' (Reality)
R. '8.'

Q. 'What action will you take to get to an 8?' (Will)
R. 'Focus on building aerobic fitness by L2 training 3x per week for 1.5 hours per session.'

Q. 'How bought into this are you? On a scale of 1 – 10... 10 being completely?' (Will)
R. '10. I start on Monday!'

Some Questions To Ask Yourself

Some people may find dartboards and mnemonics aren't their thing – here's a more general set of questions to ask yourself which will still allow you to focus your improvement (and even set goals!).

QUESTION	YOUR ANSWER
How do you rate yourself as a paddler compared to where you want to be?	
How would you like to see your paddling improve over the next year?	
Which area would you prioritise?	
What would be the measures of improvement?	
What is the first thing about this area you would work on?	
Where are you now in this area?	
Where would you want to be by the end of the training period?	
What actions will you take to get to this level?	
What resources will you use in terms of time, help and equipment?	
When do you intend to start?	
How bought into this are you?	
What level will you be at in two months time?	

You can download this table from www.fernhurstbooks.com – search for 'Improving Your Stand Up Paddleboarding' and click on 'Additional Resources'

SUMMARY

Improvement is about amassing experience. You need to push yourself at times beyond your comfort zone. You need patience and appreciate that improvement occurs in bursts. Be clear about what you are aiming for. Every time you go out on the water, have a clear goal to focus on.

Use coaching methods to support your improvement journey. Come back to your goals every two months, or so, to gauge your progress.

Enjoyment is always the ultimate goal. If you are not enjoying the challenges you have set yourself, take time to reflect on your priorities. It's possible they have become confused. This is your journey – keep it that way!

CHAPTER 2

IMPROVE YOUR EFFICIENCY

Efficiency is the ability to get optimum speed and distance from minimal input

WHAT DO WE MEAN BY EFFICIENCY?

Have you ever been paddling with someone who appears to be putting far less effort into their stroke than you are, yet they are going at an equal or greater speed? You are digging into the water with each stroke, searching for an extra litre of oxygen per breath, and they just seemingly dance along, ready at any moment for polite conversation. Your board tips as you shift weight between feet as you change sides. There is a fumble as your bottom hand goes to the handle of your paddle, and you miss a stroke in the process. Your board surges and then slows between strokes. Your blade splashes as it hits the water and again as it leaves. Your body starts to sway as you tire, your head is slumped forward, your arms feel fatigued and your legs tremble.

Meanwhile, their board remains perfectly flat; their paddle knifes the water cleanly before each clean catch and exits with the slightest splash. They seem to get twice the glide, yet everything appears seamless, calm and smooth. Their posture never changes, and their rhythm remains metronomic. Their balance is untroubled, with their head located directly over their body and the board's centreline. They always seem to have time to scan the environment for waves, boats and weather conditions. Welcome to the world of the efficient paddler.

Efficiency is the holy grail of professional athletes, particularly in disciplines such as long-distance running. Sports scientists continuously study the relationship between optimal stride length, cadence (stride rate) and leg strength. Pause for thought and compare the complexity of paddling with that of running. There are more external variables to contend with in paddling, and the physical movements are more demanding. Paddling is intrinsically inefficient. Therefore, every paddler needs to know what factors contribute to efficiency.

Efficiency is about doing more with the paddle and board with the feeling of less effort. Improving efficiency is an opportunity open to everyone who stands on a SUP.

An efficient paddler exerts less effort for a better result

THE BENEFITS OF BEING EFFICIENT

Efficiency is beneficial in the following ways:

Safety: Many paddlers will have experienced a situation where conditions suddenly change. Perhaps encountering a sudden squall, they find it increasingly difficult to proceed. In such situations, a more efficient stroke might make all the difference between making it home or finding themselves being foil wrapped by the local lifeguard a few miles out to sea.

Racing and long-distance: An efficient paddler becomes particularly evident in racing: they tend to pass fellow competitors in the last quarter of a race and have more in reserve for sprints and changes of pace. They enjoy (rather than endure) the race and finish with a smile on their face.

Increased range capability: An efficient paddling style will contribute substantially to the range capability of anyone going SUP touring. This helps them broaden the scope of their adventures in a safe, confident manner.

More 'in the tank' when required: For example, when downwinding, paddlers need to exert discrete bursts of energy to catch bumps. Efficiency enables a paddler to conserve energy and then tap into explosive power when required. Superior awareness of the sea can help them find opportunities to get the board to glide sometimes hundreds of metres without using a single paddle stroke.

More social: Efficient paddlers can go out with a broader range of people and match the pace of the group. They can engage in conversation rather than having to put all their effort into paddling.

Being an efficient paddler means that you can match the pace of others and be more social

EFFICIENCY STEMS FROM AWARENESS

When paddling, two natural systems are constantly interacting with each other:

■ The first system is **human**. This system is complex and consists of body, mind and soul.

■ The other system is the **environment** which consists of all things water (e.g. waves, tides, eddies, rebounds), the wind, the local topography and, at times, other humans. This system is also highly complex and offers an ever-changing set of challenges.

When paddling, there are two natural systems constantly interacting with each other and interfacing through the board & paddle

The interface between the two systems is the board and paddle. When paddling, the senses constantly process information to read the ongoing situation. This happens both through the conscious and unconscious mind. The body then continuously adapts the board and paddle to the inputs received by the senses. What is taking place is utterly incredible. It is something far more complex than the firing of neurotransmitters and the movement of muscles. This ever-changing dynamic makes SUP fascinating and challenging. Humans have an inbuilt desire to conquer adversity and succeed at something they perceive as problematic.

Through experience and by continuously getting out of their comfort zone, paddlers gain more feel for the stroke and the glide of the board. They learn to read the conditions with intuition rather than conscious thought. They become 'unconsciously competent'. This is the key to entering the feeling of 'flow' (see Chapter 8). They will have moved through stages of being consciously incompetent and consciously competent to get there (see P9). The feeling of being in flow is both spiritual and physical. It's a feeling of being alive and being integrated into nature. It is almost zen-like and stems from deep states of awareness.

Awareness is a crucial attribute of an **efficient** paddler. They will use their senses continuously to observe the body's movements, the board and the paddle, and act accordingly.

An efficient paddler will be aware of themselves, the board and paddle and their environment

THE HABITS OF THE INEFFICIENT PADDLER

Meanwhile, **inefficient** paddlers do some or all of the following:

- Allow the board to **rock** from side to side by shifting body weight when changing paddle hand. When this happens, the side with more weight digs into the water, creating an imbalance in drag. There is a slowing of the board on that side and a resultant loss in course direction. This also presents a higher risk of falling into the water.
- Allow the board to **tip** excessively front to back. The paddler does not move their feet to compensate, causing the board to pitch into the waves in front, creating stalling. This slows the board drastically. This can occur both heading into waves and going with the waves.
- Stand with their head **in front** of (instead of above) their body. There is now a force with a component acting opposite to where they want to go. This force will slow them down.
- Paddle **offline**: because they direct the blade in such a way that it does not propel them 'straight', they lose distance every stroke.
- Do not change paddle hands very quickly, causing missed strokes and excessive slowing of the board.
- Do not twist the paddle at the release, slowing the board glide.
- Do not feather the blade during recovery, which increases the energy required to produce the stroke and inhibits cadence.
- Waste forward energy by pushing their backsides backwards in the power phase.
- Fall off their boards more frequently than others.
- Adopt an uncomfortable posture, such as hunched back and shoulders that can increase lower or higher back pain.
- Build too much tension in the feet, creating numbness or pain.
- Adopt straight legs making the stance uncomfortable and unstable in choppier conditions.

While all these things might seem minor, paddling is an incremental activity. An hour's paddling is comprised of literally thousands of individual strokes. If each stroke has inbuilt inefficiency, these individual errors are therefore amplified by a factor of thousands.

Paddle not vertical, causing the board to go sideways thereby losing forward propulsion

Paddler has their head too far beyond their body, causing an unstable stance

Example Of The Effect Of Inefficiency

In the following example, assume the paddler has:

- An average stroke distance of **3m** (i.e. the distance the board goes per stroke is 3m)
- A paddle rate of **44 strokes** per minute

This means that, over an hour, they would expect to cover a distance of:

60 minutes x 44 strokes per minute x 3m per stroke = 7920m = 7.9km

Issue 1: In each paddle stroke, they paddle at an angle of 13 degrees to the intended line. This means they are losing **0.1m** per stroke to the line they want to follow.

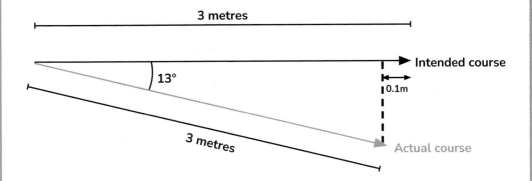

Issue 2: They stand with their head ahead of the body, thereby creating an opposing force acting against their intended direction. This could reduce their distance per stroke by another **0.1m** per stroke.

Issue 3: They miss 2 strokes (through poor changeover) per minute which means they lose **6m** distance per minute.

These errors add together meaning a loss of:

Issue 1:	0.1m per stroke x 60 minutes x 44 strokes per minute	= 264m
Issue 2:	0.1m per stroke x 60 minutes x 44 strokes per minute	= 264m
Issue 3:	6m per minute x 60 minutes	= 360m
	Total lost distance = 888m	= 0.9km

So the actual distance they would travel is:

7.9km – 0.9km = 7km

If they could correct these errors they would travel **13%** further in the same time!

AREAS TO IMPROVE EFFICIENCY

Become More Stable On The Board

Stability is a cornerstone of SUP enjoyment. It also plays a significant role in being efficient. When a paddler falls in the water, they unsettle themselves. This inevitably leads to a loss of rhythm, energy and confidence. So stability and efficiency are inextricably linked. Stability stems from several factors:

The board: Board width influences stability. Paddlers often believe that narrower is faster. While this is true if an outboard motor is attached to the back of the board, it is not true when humans provide the power. Without stability, a paddler cannot exert a powerful stroke. Without a powerful stroke, the paddler is neither stable nor particularly successful. We will look into this in more detail in Chapter 7 concerning equipment. Paddlers should never sacrifice stability in the quest for speed.

The position of the feet on the board: Some paddlers prefer offset feet; others prefer in-line. The argument for offset stems from the world of martial arts. It is argued that offset provides more planes of stability than in-line. This makes sense, and most accomplished paddlers adopt a degree of offset. But there are exceptions to this, so it seems to be a personal choice. Experiment to find your preferred strategy. Here are some suggestions:

- Place your feet slightly back from the centreline when heading into waves. This will allow the board's nose to ride over the oncoming water easier.
- Place your feet slightly forward of the centreline when going with the waves and when just coming out of the trough of a wave. This will help to 'trap' the board onto the emerging wave that is coming behind you before it crests.
- Place your feet further forward in side winds to prevent the wind force from rotating the board away from your intended direction.
- Offset your feet to enable some 'foot' steering when downwinding.

An offset stance helps you to steer with your feet and gain a better sense of the movements of the board

Itzel Delgado in downwind action: his feet are behind the centreline as he is focussing on keeping the nose out of the water'

How the paddle is used: The best paddlers use the paddle to keep themselves on the board. Other paddlers just use it to move the board. The paddle should be used as a brace, a steering device, a counterweight and a means of propulsion.

Strength and flexibility: Stability is founded on strong legs and a flexible body. Stiff ankles and a body that is not capable of rapid compensations consign paddlers to the water – particularly in unstable conditions. Undertaking a fitness regime that includes a variety of squats can dramatically improve leg strength. The benefits of stronger legs can be instantly felt out on the water. We will look at this in more detail in Chapter 5 concerning physicality. A strong core facilitates power, and stability is directly proportional to the power of the stroke.

Application of technique: When conditions are manageable, technique can be relatively easy to apply. When conditions become challenging, technique becomes more essential but at the same time, more difficult to apply. A lower body position (by adopting more bent legs and a head that stays up and above the body) provides a stable base. (Technique is covered in the next chapter.)

Using the paddle to brace

29

Fiona Wylde shows bent legs and low stance to gain stability and speed

Unstable stance with legs stiff and straight

Confidence and calm: The mind and body are part of the same system. Our bodies and our movement reflect our mental state. If we are fearful, then our bodies adopt a flight response. The flight response is about removing ourselves from the situation rather than facing it. This is not a resourceful mindset to meet challenging conditions on the water! A paddler will not perform to the best of their ability by feeling fearful. Worse still, feelings of fear

can be habituated by repeated failure. Such a mindset must be broken through self-reflection and visualisation. Confidence and calm are the only ways to maintain consistent stability. It is possible to reprogramme our response to a challenging situation.

Here is one approach based on Neuro-Linguistic Programming which involves visualisation. Find a quiet place with some undisturbed time:

- Practise some deep abdominal breathing to relax.
- Close your eyes and visualise the challenging situation and see yourself within it.
- Experience the emotions as if you were there. Examine these emotions and detect the signs of fear and doubt.
- Deep breathe to wipe out this memory by picturing it as a photograph, then rubbing it out in your mind's eye (or scribbling over it with a Sharpie pen).
- Revisualise the same situation.
- This time see yourself excelling in the environment. Perhaps smiling or shouting with excitement. Feel the emotions of confidence and joy running through your mind and body. Feel the difference in your confidence and see the improvement in your physical actions – the stroke, balance and general body language.
- Rewind the scene as many times as necessary to anchor feelings of joy and confidence into the situation. Play some dynamic music to reinforce these positive feelings.
- If it helps, create a physical trigger on your body that you can access to remind you of these feelings. This will need to be something that you can do at the time of stress – so it might be something like pushing the tongue into the roof of the mouth. You can also play the music in your mind when it's needed to flood your mind with confident feelings.

A relaxed mind creates a relaxed body: Tightness inhibits performance in any sporting arena. A successful SUP stroke requires considerable extension, rotation and contraction. None of these physical actions can be done to their best without relaxation. Stability is best achieved through well-executed technique and a responsive body. In contrast, stress promotes stiffness which leads to an inability to adapt the body to sudden changes in direction.

How the fin is used: The fin is a critical component of the paddleboard. A smaller fin increases glide but reduces stability, while a longer fin increases stability but reduces glide. Being able to vary fin types to the conditions improves the opportunities for efficiency. In a similar vein, the location of the fin will affect performance. Placing the fin near the front of the fin box improves the ease of turning. Placing the fin at the back improves straight-line tracking. Therefore deliberately choosing the fin location for specific tasks will pay dividends. A beach race with many buoy turns will require a fin location at the front of the box. A 16km downwinder will not. (For more details on fins, see Chapter 7.)

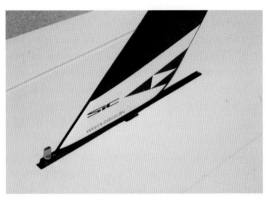

Fin at the front of box for fast turns

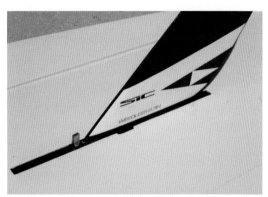

Fin at the back of box for optimal tracking and few or no turns

Fin in the middle for some turns and some tracking

Increase The Sensory Acuity

Sensory acuity is the ability to take in inputs from the environment and respond accordingly. Such behaviour does not require conscious thought and can be developed just like a muscle through purposeful exercise. Walking down the street on a Sunday morning to get a morning latte does not require masses of sensory acuity. The environment is predictable and relatively static. Stand on a board and paddle in a 35-knot downwind with a 3m swell behind you, and the senses need to be dialled up. Paddling in such conditions will rely on constantly processing inputs related to sight, sound and feel.

Some paddlers might depend primarily on their visual sense. In that case, they may build additional acuity by practising a switch of attention to their feet. Stand one-legged on the ground and contrast your performance between having eyes open and eyes closed. If eyes closed is much more difficult, spend more time practising balancing with your eyes closed. The objective is to increase your sensitivity to the non-visual inputs.

Standing one-legged with your eyes closed improves your sense of balance

Develop More Awareness Of The Water Patterns

Wind and waves show themselves on the surface of the sea. The more a paddler studies the way water behaves, the better equipped they will be to make advantageous choices.

Choosing a route: Sometimes, it is pertinent not to take the most direct route from A to B. It is easier to paddle directly into both wind or waves than at 90 degrees to them. Experienced paddlers will sometimes choose an indirect route to manage difficult situations. Inexperienced ones will try to go direct and suffer the consequences.

Understand the origin of water patterns: Patterns emerge on any water surface. The more you understand the roots of these patterns, the more able you will be to use them to your advantage. For example, on the sea, you will often see multiple patterns. These might consist of swell waves, wind waves and rebound waves.

Swell waves might originate from tens or even hundreds of miles away. Generally, these will have a longer wave length than other waves and move relatively quickly. There might be multiple swell waves coming from different directions. These will cause interference patterns as they converge.

Wind waves will originate from more local conditions and go in the direction of the prevailing wind. They will have a smaller amplitude and generally move slower than the bigger swell waves.

Rebound waves occur when the swell, or the wind waves, hit a hard surface such as rocks or cliffs. These then produce more waves that radiate out from the point of impact. These can be confusing to observe as they will create interference. However, they offer an opportunity for a ride, and skilled paddlers will actively seek them out along the coastline.

Anyone interested in developing their awareness in this area should take time to sit and watch the emerging patterns on the sea.

This can also be done in other bodies of water, such as lakes and rivers. All these environments create water patterns that a paddler must be aware of. We explore more on this subject in Chapter 6.

The larger swell waves which have been driven over long distances

See the small wind waves brushing on the top of the sea

Rebound waves bounce back when a wave hits a surface

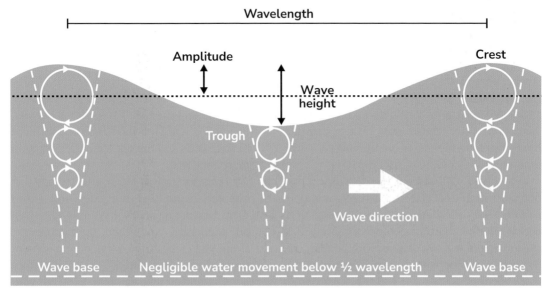

Anatomy of a wave: water within a wave moves in a circular motion

Choosing waves: We will look at this in more detail in Chapter 5 in the downwinding section. Efficient paddlers choose the waves that have the biggest payoff. Sometimes this will mean choosing the smaller wind waves and not the predominant swell waves. The wind waves will probably be easier to catch and be more frequent, making them easier to 'stitch' together to create a continuous 'ride'. Catching larger waves might be more exhilarating, but it might be less efficient as they will cost more energy to acquire.

Furthermore, they might cause the rider to pitch and slow as they constantly accelerate into the slower waves ahead of them. Experienced downwinders will process the terrain of waves around them to make the best choices. Paddlers who look similar on the flat can soon be differentiated when they face conditions requiring knowledge of water patterns.

Keep The Board Moving

Most people have probably studied or heard of Newton's Law of Motion. Based on physical observation, the 17th Century mathematician Sir Isaac Newton, devised mathematical equations that correlate with the way physical bodies move on our planet.

When we paddle, we convert chemical energy (generally derived from food) to kinetic energy (associated with movement). For the board to move, we must overcome a variable resistance of fluids in the form of wind and water, called drag. These counter forces increase the faster we go and can vary dramatically according to conditions.

The board's movement involves using our bodies to apply a set of forces on the submerged paddle. This is called the power phase and occurs over a short time (approximately 0.5 seconds). In a journey of 9km, with an average distance of 3m per stroke, a paddler will make 3,000 strokes.

Each stroke creates a force on the paddle directed downwards (to provide lift to the board) and a force directed in the opposite direction to where we wish to go. The force downwards is felt by a lifting of the front of the board. This lifting reduces the friction that exists between the board and water because we are, in effect, making the board lighter. Skilled paddlers will use some of their body weight to produce a downward force on the paddle.

The force related to moving forwards is felt in the feet (as they are the only part of our body in contact with the board). We use energy generated in the whole body to drive the feet past the paddle. We use the blade to trap a volume of water that acts as an 'anchor' to pull ourselves past.

Each paddler must find the best fit between the forces associated with lift and forward motion. Too much lift, and we bounce the board on each stroke. Too little, and we get 'glued' to the water. Finding the optimum balance between the two can only be achieved by feeling. It can frequently change due to different conditions. Because force is directional and we are applying multi-directional forces, we call the sum of these forces an 'impulse'.

After each impulse, we immediately start to slow down for two reasons:

- Drag associated with water exists between all the surfaces of the board that are in contact with the water. These surfaces include the underside, the rails, the nose and the tail. If the rider is heavier, the board will sink further, creating more surface area to contact water, resulting in more friction.
- Air resistance also has a role to play. Air hits the board and the rider and slows them down. On windy days this force can be significant and even unmanageable. Even when there is no wind, our movement forward is subjected to drag from surrounding air (like you feel if you put your hand out of a moving car window).

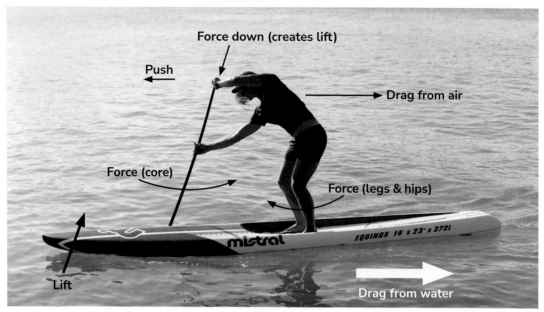

The forces involved in moving a board

So, even when there is little or no wind, and we are paddling on flat water, the drag forces are still considerable.

The drag and air resistance equations are complex, but suffice it to say, they are significant. You can judge for yourself by taking 1 stroke from a standstill and seeing how quickly you slow down. Water has a high surface tension (second only to mercury in all known fluids), making it feel 'sticky'. It grabs at the board, the fin and the paddle. Introduce some waves and a headwind, and the energy required to maintain a moderate speed is considerable.

Kinetic energy is the energy a body has by virtue of movement. It is defined as $\frac{1}{2}mv^2$ where:

- m = mass of the body in kg
- v = velocity in metres per second

From this formula, we see that the kinetic energy of a moving board is related to the square of the velocity. The kinetic energy of a board and rider going at 5km/h (1.39m/s) versus one travelling at 10km/h (2.78m/s) is different by a factor of 4:

$$1.39 \times 1.39 = 1.93$$
$$2.78 \times 2.78 = 7.73$$
$$7.73 \div 1.93 = 4.0$$

The rider travelling twice as fast requires 4 times the energy input. And the actual energy differential is more than this because it ignores the fact that drag forces increase as speed increases.

Keeping things simple, this also means that if you allow your speed to drop from 10km/h (2.78m/s) to 5km/h (1.39 m/s), you need to input considerably more than twice the energy to get back than if you only drop to 7.5km/h (2.08m/s).

You can immediately see the importance of conserving speed to avoid having to make significant energy inputs at every stroke.

Some athletes can maintain a powerful stroke for extended periods. Their stroke will tend to be longer, deeper and operate at a relatively slow cadence (stroke frequency). Most people are not blessed with the physical ability to do this. Consequently, they should consider increasing their cadence to maintain velocity and 'keep the board moving'.

Develop Bodily Awareness

Bruce Lee (a martial arts expert) was famous for delivering a one-inch punch. He could floor a man with virtually no body movement or wind up. The forces generated at his fist were astounding. He claimed that his right-handed punch started in his left foot and then coordinated energy through his entire body into his fist. You are blessed with a body that can store and release energy in this manner.

Paddling is a complex series of movements that takes place over a short period requiring the participation of the entire body. Every action must be coordinated to amplify and transfer energy to the feet. Inefficient paddlers don't use all the power they have at their disposal. Furthermore, they 'dissipate' the energy they do have through uncoordinated movements.

They need to 'feel' what parts of the body are engaged during the stroke. They also need to recognise what parts are not engaging and question whether this is desirable. Common 'engagement' faults include:

- The omission of the abs, obliques and lats during the pull
- The non-use of the hips and legs near the end of the power phase

Bodily awareness can be developed through specific training exercises, such as:

Paddle with the handle in the water: This gives us a much less efficient paddle. Discover how much more the legs want to get involved in driving the board forwards in this situation.

Paddling with the handle in the water (less efficient paddle) means the legs need to get more involved

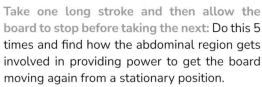
Take one long stroke and then allow the board to stop before taking the next: Do this 5 times and find how the abdominal region gets involved in providing power to get the board moving again from a stationary position.

Paddle with loose arms and hands: Feel how the core comes in to compensate for the loss of involvement in the arms.

Paddle slowly over 5km and focus on particular parts of the body over this distance: Dedicate at least 2 minutes per body area to ascertain what is being felt in that area. Feel the way the various parts of the body connect in a chain reaction to produce power. Paddle extra slowly or in an exaggerated manner to amplify sensations.

The more 'bodily aware' a paddler can become, the more able they will be to improve their technique.

Increase Cadence

Cadence is simply your stroke rate. It is usually measured in strokes per minute. If you have a Garmin or similar GPS watch, there is usually a facility to measure stroke rate offered in the SUP menu. Paddlers will have a preferred rate that feels comfortable for them.

Several factors will affect the cadence they adopt:

The physical characteristics of the paddler: A taller, more physically powerful paddler may feel more comfortable with longer, deeper strokes. A shorter or less powerful paddler may feel more comfortable with a faster stroke rate. They achieve a quicker rate by their physical dimensions (shorter arms, legs and paddle length) and take a shorter stroke.

The type of board: The longer the board, the more the glide per stroke. Therefore it is possible to reduce your cadence with a longer board and still achieve similar speeds to when you are paddling with a higher cadence on a shorter board.

The personality of the paddler: Some people appear more languid than others. Their

Example of how cadence can compensate for a lack of physical strength

Paddler 1 is a strong young man at the peak of his physical fitness. His average distance per stroke is 3.5m. His average stroke rate is 48 strokes per min.

Paddler 2 is not as strong as P1. She cannot generate the same power per stroke over any prolonged period of time. But she is super fit and can maintain a high cadence. Her average stroke distance is 3m, P2's stroke rate is 56 strokes per min.

How do their speeds compare?
Paddler 1: 3.5m x 48 strokes per minute = 168m per minute = 2.8m/s = 10km/hr
Paddler 2: 3m x 56 strokes per minute = 168 m per minute = 2.8m/s = 10km/hr

nature off the water is often reflected in how they paddle on the water (and, therefore their cadence).

The size of the paddle blade: A big blade area will grab more water than a smaller one. This will generate more power per stroke but be more energy-sapping to use. So generally, big bladed paddles promote low cadence paddling. However, this is not always the case, as we will discover in the next chapter by examining Bruno Hasulyo's stroke.

Conditions: A high cadence may be desirable in certain conditions. For example, a paddler might feel more stable with a faster stroke. Or sometimes, a paddler might need to rest certain muscles and revert to a shorter, quicker stroke.

Habit: Cadence becomes set through habit. Sometimes paddlers can benefit by challenging this habit. This can be done by dramatically changing the stroke rate during a paddle. A slow cadence is a stroke rate below 44 strokes per minute, medium is 45 to 55, and high is above 55.

This paddler chokes down on the paddle to gain high cadence

CONCLUSIONS

Paddlers need to find a rhythm that suits them and the conditions. It is a pace that perfectly balances stroke rate, stroke power and board glide. This is what we call 'paddling resonance'.

Many paddlers do not focus enough on being efficient, preferring to search for additional power. But developing an 'efficiency' mindset is the first step toward improvement.

In this chapter, we have looked at many factors that influence efficiency and suggested how efficiency can be gained.

Efficiency is founded on cultivating a continual awareness of how the board behaves, the body feels and the environment changes.

Before you move on, consider the content of this chapter and ask yourself how 'efficiency aware' you are at the moment. You might like to use the dartboard below. Then consider what actions you will take to develop this mindset further.

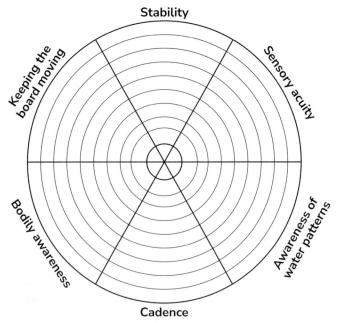

An efficiency mindset dartboard
You can download this dartboard and blank ones from www.fernhurstbooks.com – search for 'Improving Your Stand Up Paddleboarding' and click on 'Additional Resources'

CHAPTER 3

IMPROVE YOUR TECHNIQUE

*Technique: a method or skill
to perform a task*

THERE IS NO RIGHT WAY

All paddlers adopt a technique. Some will have been taught, but most develop their 'method' from 'trial and error' and the observation of others. Visual clues offer only part of the story of any paddle stroke. Watching tells you nothing about what the other person is thinking or feeling as they execute the stroke. Consequently, you can attempt to copy someone else's methods and not get the same results.

When a coach or a friend offers advice, it is usually based on a personal ideal. These are built on the culmination of their personal experience and the 'accepted' wisdom they subscribe to.

The first people to adopt SUP were from a canoeing background. Good technique was primarily defined by maximum rotation, long reach and a deep, powerful stroke. This suited a particular physical build and mindset.

More recently, paddlers with no reference to the likes of the OC1 canoe have challenged these ideas. Watch a pro SUP race now and you will see a variety of styles adopted by riders who all compete closely for the podium. The 'accepted' method has given way to 'what works best for the individual'.

There has been an emergent process as paddlers have experimented and changed their approach accordingly. You must learn to do this if you intend to improve your stroke. Don't get too hung up on having a 'correct' stroke. Expect to change your stroke regularly as you develop a greater sense of feel for what works for you.

Various Factors Influence A Paddler's Technique

References: Established kayakers and canoeists have very different references to surfers. Both of these groups have substantially different references to a newcomer totally inexperienced in watersports.

Physical attributes: Physical stature will undoubtedly affect the application of technique. Factors such as height, build and body shape will affect the method adopted.

Knowledge: This is acquired by undertaking a task and reflecting on the result. To gain knowledge, you need to be exposed to new experiences. This can be challenging at times but necessary for progress.

Skill: Skill is the ability to apply knowledge successfully. Developing a skill requires practice, patience, success and confidence.

Attitude: Attitude is the degree of determination or intention someone has to do something. Paddling is rewarding, but improvement requires time and a particular mindset. Improving has to matter to someone; otherwise, it won't happen. If someone is happy with their technique, they won't change it.

LOADING UP TO CREATE FORCE

Before exploring the SUP paddle stroke in detail, it is worth looking at things from a macro point of view. It is helpful to consider other sports where an athlete loads their body to create directed force.

Golf: The golf swing comprises a wind-up (the backswing), a pause, a downswing, an impact and a follow-through. The clubhead travels at a remarkable 120mph when it hits the ball. This is achieved through the coiling and uncoiling of the body. The golfer creates incredible speed by creating tension between the upper and lower part of their body. The lower moves ahead of the upper to create

A good golf swing has a balance of relaxation coupled with power

tension, similar to stretching an elastic band between the fingers. There is then perfect timing at impact to harvest this elastic energy. A good golf swing has tempo and a balance of relaxation coupled with power.

Standing jump: To get maximum height out of a standing jump, the athlete uses their upper body to push their feet down into the floor. This creates the storage of energy. This energy travels downwards and then upwards to enable the feet to leave the floor like a spring. The athlete uses their upper body to maximise the height gained. There is a storage of energy, an explosive change of direction and a release. The height jumped will be much reduced if the athlete does not drop down first and does not use their upper body to generate energy. There is a dynamic between relaxation and stiffness. The athlete relaxes into stored energy. They then stiffen at the point the energy is applied to the floor, before relaxing the body again to allow the energy to be fully expressed and not wasted through any tension.

See how the athlete stores energy by pushing into the ground first

Karate punch: The punch is based on creating power from twisting. Twisting forces are called torsion, and the human body is well equipped to generate such forces. The karate punch relies on relaxation to store energy, a rapid change of direction to create acceleration, full-body engagement to develop maximum power, bodily stiffness at the point of impact and a release after impact. Anyone who attempts to be 'strong' throughout the punch appears stiff and cannot achieve the forces and speed of an accomplished black belt.

In all these examples, the athlete stores energy by moving the body in the opposite direction to the one they intend to go. The stages are storage, pause, return, impact and, finally, release. The body is only 'stiff' during impact.

Imagine you are standing on your paddleboard without a paddle. How would you move it forwards from a standing position? The only way would be by using your body to create effective movements in your feet. Try it and feel what we mean.

It is possible to generate board movement (in a standing position) without a paddle or access to external instruments. Notice the wind up of the body and the need to stiffen to initiate the board's movement.

Now imagine you are standing on your board, and this time there are two guide wires on either side of you within easy reach of your hands. (A bit like you might find on a pedestrian bridge over a ravine.) Imagine the way you would use your body to drive the board forwards while you hold the guidewires. You would probably reach forward as far as you could, bending at the hips and then use your core and legs to drive the board forward.

Next, imagine you are standing on the board, but there is only one guidewire on the right-hand side. Imagine how you would use your body to move forward now. Your right hand would reach forward and pull on the wire. You would hinge at the hips to get as long a reach as possible. Your core would work extra hard to fight the urge that the board would now have to rotate towards the right. Your core would probably twist away from the wire to get extra power. You might stand offset on the board to the fight it veering offline.

All three of these visualisations are helpful to illustrate the role of the hips, the core and the legs in generating motion.

It is possible to move the board forward without using a paddle by bending the knees and straightening up

THE STAGES OF THE PADDLE STROKE

Let us take a look at the stages of the paddle stroke and offer a commentary on the sensations we encounter through the five stages:

1. Set-up
2. Catch
3. Power phase
4. Exit
5. Recovery

1. The Set-Up

This is the part of the stroke where the body becomes loaded with energy. This takes place through coiling and / or springing the body and setting the paddle in the air before inserting it into the water.

In this picture, note the position of the hands, the twist of the body, flex of legs. Check out the stance. The paddler has bent legs, with their weight evenly distributed over the feet. There is a definite angle along the line from lower back to back of the head. See how the high top hand creates potential energy. See the rotation in the shoulders and how the core is turned. This is all stored energy waiting to be released.

At this stage, the paddler will feel some tension across their abdominals, back muscles and chest (all of which have twisted out of their usual plane and want to return to neutral).

The set-up

The lower arm extends not entirely straight, while the top arm remains high. The hands are stacked above each other. The paddle is held at a positive angle to the water surface. The length of reach can be increased (if required) by rotating the hips and the upper body more, or bringing the top hand closer to the rest of the body. The paddle-side knee bends.

Doing these actions enables the blade to hover above the water at an increased distance from the paddler's body. Some paddlers believe that the more distance, the better. Others think that there is an optimum position. You can experiment to determine what is right for you. The more reach, the longer the stroke. The more twisting and hingeing, the more potential power, but also the more unstable the paddler becomes.

The set-up will dictate the type and quality of stroke you will perform.

The set-up with maximum twist, giving a longer reach

The set-up with less twist and less reach

2. The Catch

The catch is where the paddler moves from setting up the blade above the water to inserting it. You must insert the blade at a positive angle, that is to say the blade is less than ninety degrees to the water at entry (see photo). This maximises the opportunity to trap water and provides essential lift. A good catch can be felt straight away. The paddle feels like it has been glued into the water. With a poor catch the blade does not fix itself in the water. Consequently, you will feel it 'flutter' as it moves backwards in the power phase.

See the blade enter the water at an angle that provides lift to the paddler

Much is said about the need for a smooth blade entry into the water. This encourages paddlers to place the blade carefully into the water. This 'placement' mindset can be to the detriment of getting the blade into the water quickly. Water has an incredibly high surface tension for a fluid – second only to mercury! You do need to use force to break this. Watch Michael Booth (the Aussie SUP powerhouse) put his paddle in the water. He crashes it in!

Our tip is to practise crashing the blade into the water and dial back from this. Ultimately you are aiming for a positive, quick entry that is clean and relatively splash-free. Use the muscles between your shoulder blades to drive the paddle into the water. You will find that by deliberately stabbing the paddle into the water, you gain instant lift and forward momentum. You also create a distinct pause between the catch and power phases. This pause creates a cue for the abdominals to tighten and support the legs in thrusting you towards the paddle.

If you struggle to stab the blade into the water (many people do) then you need to work on getting the blade in as quickly and cleanly as possible. This is more difficult than it seems, because your brain is often desperate to initiate the power phase. Therefore, many paddlers do not complete a (full and deep) catch before they initiate the 'pull' and their stroke is compromised. The difference in timing is perhaps tenths of a second. The difference in the resultant stroke is vast.

Michael Booth preparing to do his aggressive catch

Angled fore and aft, but vertical looking from ahead if you want to go straight

A good catch is absolutely essential for power and stability

Top paddlers find different ways to use their bodies to get the paddle into the water quickly. For example, Ty Judson is a proponent of hinging at the hips to drop his body weight onto the paddle to effect a fast, powerful catch.

If you intend to go straight, the paddle must be vertical (when looking from ahead) at the catch. If it goes into the water at an angle you will be putting a rotational force on the paddle causing you to move sideways. If you actually do want to direct the board off the straight line, then a non-vertical paddle will deliver a turning action.

The out-to-in stroke is the most fundamental stroke in SUP. It involves placing the paddle away from the nose of the board and bringing it towards your feet. Your set-up creates a successful out-to-in stroke. You need to visualise a point where you want the blade the enter and exit the board. It's not fancy, but it is practical. This stroke enables you to maintain a straight line and compensate for turning forces on the board. It's importance is highlighted when you encounter strong side winds and have to exaggerate the action to maintain a straight course. If you don't master this skill you will find yourself in certain conditions having to paddle exclusively on one side – something that is very difficult to physically maintain.

3. Power Phase

There are different ways of switching the power on in the power phase. It is not feasible or desirable for most paddlers to only use one particular set of muscles for an extended period of time. Every paddler's body is different, and their ability to create power will reflect these differences. The task is to optimise your resources and avoid exhaustion or injury.

The power phase only lasts half a second and provides most of the impulse to drive the board forward. What you feel in the power phase will depend on the stroke you are performing and the muscle groups you are using.

The main muscle groups you will use are the lats (lattissimus dorsi muscle), abdominals, obliques, shoulders, rhomboids, hips, glutes, quads, triceps, biceps and the many muscles in the feet. Yes, it's quite a collection! If you generally finish a paddle session with sore arms you are not engaging these muscle groups sufficiently!

You will use these muscles to different degrees and in different sequences depending on the intended stroke and your physical make up. What you are seeking to do is to ensure the largest muscles take on most of the load. The way you coordinate the firing of the muscle groups will determine how well you succeed in driving the board forwards with each stroke.

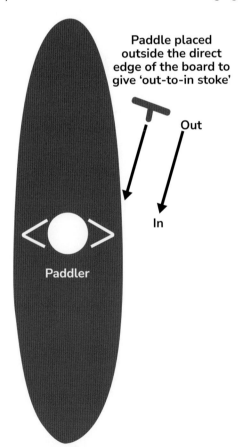

Paddle placed outside the direct edge of the board to give 'out-to-in stoke'

Out

In

Paddler

The out-to-in stroke, the fundamental directional stroke to master

If you have perfected the spearing action, you can obtain some useful forward momentum at the catch phase. This makes this approach perfect for catching waves and obtaining immediate acceleration. Once the blade is locked in the water you naturally thrust your body forwards using primarily your abs, glutes, legs and feet.

This approach is physically demanding and most 'average' paddlers cannot sustain the spearing action for long time periods. Consequently, they revert to 'placing' the paddle in the water. This is less dynamic and less energy-sapping.

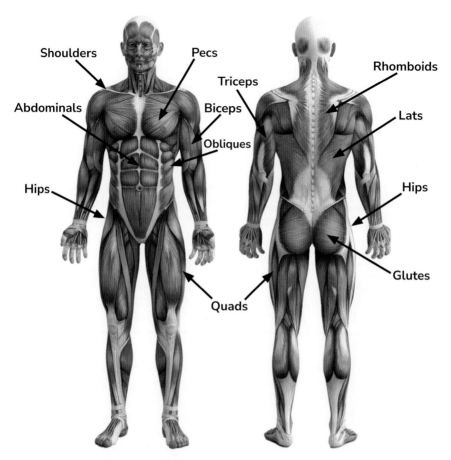

The key SUP muscles and body parts

Here are some of the physical sensations you might experience in the power phase with a less dynamic catch. Please note we use the word 'might' because we have discovered that each paddler seems to engage different muscle groups at this stage. You will need to experiment and determine whether you are engaging the areas you want (or need) to. Remember, your whole body is available to be used in this phase.

The rhomboid muscles are used to push the paddle down in a vertical direction. A split second later, the lower hand tightens on the shaft and initiates the pull, but the corresponding lat does the pull. (Consciously focus on the lat pulling rather than your bicep, otherwise fatigue in your arms will set in quickly.) The lats are a primary paddling instrument for many as the big meaty masses of muscle are powerful and do not fatigue easily. The oblique muscles on the same side also activate at the same time to stiffen the core.

As the pull proceeds, there is a point where the top hand will rotate over the bottom hand. Then, the top hand's lats and obliques become dominant force contributors and they push the top handle away from the body. You may feel your pecs contract to help with the top hand push. At the same time the hips will uncoil and 'flick' back to square acting as an extra force to pull the blade back.

The legs (bent and poised) provide a forward thrust before the blade exits. The force from the legs is created by both the glutes and the quads. These are the largest muscle groups in the body and are both durable and best equipped to create a sudden impulse on the board. The legs absorb all the energy stored by the upper body and use it to force the feet forward.

The resultant feeling is 'power without strain'.

Please note that the application of power on the paddle is predominantly downwards. This downward force is created by the muscles in the back and the hinging of the hips. The lateral force (what many people consider the pull) is generally less significant in magnitude than the downward force. The blade should go deep – so that only the shaft is visible in the water. Many less experienced paddlers try to generate more lateral force than downward force and lose the 'up lift' that is important for breaking the significant drag forces associated with water.

Some paddlers seem to be able to switch the power on quicker than others – meaning they get the power into the blade early. Others gain power through the stroke. This may well relate to their physique and muscle fibre composition (see P85).

The position of the bottom hand provides the opportunity to gain power through leverage. The lower this hand, the greater the lever, and, therefore the more ability to create a higher force.

Power is derived from the whole body working in a connected sequence

4. Exit

At the exit, the blade needs to be taken out in a way that does not create a stopping force on the board. The top hand twists outwards, the bottom hand rotates inwards and you lift the blade from the water. Some paddlers drop the upper shoulder and take the blade to a horizontal position. In contrast, others keep the blade in a vertical plane which allows for a faster recovery – especially into the wind. The 'shoulder drop' is slower but more rhythmical and provides an opportunity to brace if required. This is a personal choice, or even use both modes depending on conditions and stroke.

Exit takes place near the feet, depending on the choice of stroke. There is debate about whether an exit past the feet starts to pull the front of the board down into the water. You should experiment with exit positions, as board type and blade angle all have an effect on the best position to exit. A shorter stroke maintains cadence, momentum and enables you to get back to the set-up quicker. A longer stroke might suit someone with a powerful build.

Shoulder remains high at exit

Shoulder drops at exit to lift the blade out of the water

5. Recovery

The recovery is a time when the body should relax. This relaxation is important for a number of reasons:

- It helps improve the glide
- It provides a rhythm for the stroke
- It is a prompt for the nervous system to say that the power has been switched off and to get ready for the next power-loading stage

Nasal breathing can help the relaxation process. Relaxation is essential as our muscles and fascia cannot extend and contract effectively without it. Relaxation provides power. Paddlers who hold themselves in continuous tension throughout all stages of the stroke are wasting energy, inhibiting the ability of their body to move and creating an unresourceful mental state.

Practise coordinating your breathing with the phases of the stroke. An 'out-breath' at the point of power seems best for most paddlers. This is similar to expelling air in a punch, where you breathe out during impact to create power and rigidity in the body.

The recovery phase requires a shift in posture from low to high, in preparation to set the paddle above the water.

The recovery phase promotes relaxation, more upright posture and the beginning of the wind up of energy

THE COMPONENTS OF A GOOD STROKE

To pull this together, we will give you two checklists. The first is the elements which we regard as essential, and the second are those which can vary to a degree depending on what works best for you.

The '**givens**' are:

- Vertical paddle with hands stacked over each other for as long as possible during the power phase
- Stiff core at the point the power is switched on
- Relaxed release to initiate a powerful wind-up
- A secure catch with the entire blade submerged in the water at a positive angle before the pull
- An 'out-to-in' stroke path to keep the board tracking straight
- High top hands at the set-up to open up the body and get a powerful insertion of blade into the water
- Use of major muscle groups synchronised into the power phase

The '**negotiable**' elements are:

- The degree of rotation
- The angle of the body
- Stance of feet
- Degree of movement of the body
- Cadence

Ensure that your hands are stacked over each other for as long as possible during the power phase

PADDLING TECHNIQUES

As we have already said, there isn't one way to paddle your SUP. Different people have different approaches and it is a matter of finding what works best for you. In fact, you should look to incorporate various methods into your stroke repertoire.

Let's look at some different actions which you can view on YouTube.

Rotation: Danny Ching

Danny comes from an OC1 canoe background which has influenced his technique. He has a powerful physique. His power in the stroke is derived from massive rotation, where his back is almost 90 degrees to the plane it started at. He turns his head to facilitate his turn.

He achieves an extensive reach and then plunges the paddle deep into the water using his body weight. His force is primary directed downward. He uses his hips to create torsion and lats with the pull. He does not push too much over the top and engages his feet at the end of the power phase. It's a fluid, elegant, almost classical, style.

Hinge From Hips: Bruno Hasulyo

Bruno has studied body biomechanics and the principles of efficiency. He knows that his build favours a high stroke rate to keep the board moving at a constant speed. His build is wiry and very elastic. He can store a lot of energy in his body by winding it up into readiness for an explosive release. He does not rotate but chooses to use a pecking motion by hingeing at the hips. This requires the entire front of his body to be a primary driving force of power with a corresponding strength in his back area after the power is complete.

Bruno literally pulls himself through the water with short strokes that finish well before his feet. The technique guarantees a high cadence and high efficiency. He uses a large area blade but does not submerge it deeper than the actual blade depth. This means that he gets a full catch but can withdraw the blade quickly for the next stroke.

Bruno Hasulyo uses the central core muscles and legs to drive the board forwards

Palanca: Dani Parres

'Palanca' is a Spanish word meaning lever. With this technique you use the paddle like a lever – similar to the way you create forces on a spade when digging. This approach is often frowned upon by professional coaches as it can encourage over use of the arms. However, when done well, coordinating with the core, it is a very efficient means of generating paddle power. It is attractive to paddlers who perhaps lack the athleticism of SUP pros as it requires less body flexibility. It is also a very stable method as there is little body sway.

Over 50's world champion, Dani Parres, uses this method extremely successfully and still competes at the highest level. Dani uses the lats to push the top of the paddle over the lower hand like a piston, achieving high cadence and quick bursts of power. It works well to catch small waves on a downwind and also as a way to alter the physical loading on the body during a long paddle.

Find Your Own Way

Which technique is the best?

There is no answer to this question, although many coaches will argue there is.

Many of the world's top paddlers incorporate aspects of each of the three approaches described above. You must ensure that you adopt certain principles, but you must also be prepared to experiment with techniques to assess the best fit for your physique. There are options, and there is no correct answer.

Do not get too obsessed with developing the perfect stroke. When you are out on the water, every stroke will differ slightly – the dynamic nature of the environment will ensure that. Ultimately you will probably develop a set of effective strokes that work for you in different situations. The key here is to adopt a mindful approach each time you paddle. What you will find is that your stroke constantly evolves as your awareness and physical capability develops.

Each paddler shows differences in technique

ADOPTING A MINDFUL PRACTICE

Going Out On Your Own

When you go out or train on your own, there is a different dynamic than when paddling with others. For some, the pressure is off, and it presents a time to try things out and enjoy the sensations of paddling. Others can almost go too far and put extra strain on their performance.

Mindful practice is about sensing your body and mind throughout every stroke. It involves feeling how your body moves, which muscles are being used, when, how the feet are feeling, what the eyes are noticing and quietening the conversation in your head!

Of course, if you attempt to focus on all these things, your mind will be overwhelmed. A good practice is to dedicate one minute per area and really feel what is going on. For example:

- If you are experimenting with your stance, identify the difference in how the board behaves with changes to the foot position
- If you are experimenting with engaging the core, paddle with the core activated and then de-activated and really feel the difference
- Paddle with the legs bent to different degrees and feel how this affects how they engage with the rest of the body

These sessions are golden opportunities to attune to your paddling body and mind.

Training & Paddling With Others

Training with others is not to be undervalued. There is a camaraderie to be gained by going out together and facing the elements. It energises and helps paddlers push themselves more than they would on their own.

Sports psychologists have found that the so-called 'worst performers' improved much faster when working with others than on their own. Something is inspiring about seeing someone you know do what you would like to do. It somehow makes it more achievable for you.

As well as inspiration, you can get support and knowledge from paddling with others. These inputs improve the learning process. You can gauge your progress against the abilities of others.

Training with others can be more effective than training on your own

Training On Dry Land

You cannot see how you paddle when you are out on the water. You cannot see the angles and positions you adopt. You can ask someone to film you, which is really useful, but you can also spend time in dry-land training. Do not underestimate the value of 'paddling' on dry land in front of a mirror or full-length window. This helps you sense which muscle groups you engage throughout the stroke and gives you a chance to check your postural angles.

Technique Drills

You can view drills on YouTube that can help you work on your technique. Drills are intended to habitualise new movements. It can be helpful to break down complex movements into more simple elements to do this effectively. These elements can then be practised slowly and individually before being knitted together at full speed. This approach has been used for centuries by martial arts disciplines. You will see karate students practice 'katas' – movements performed slowly to help the conscious mind sense the feelings that would otherwise be unregistered at full speed.

Drills that we would recommend everyone undertake regularly are as follows:

1. Paddle with the handle in the water

A fantastic way to force the engagement of the legs and reduce the involvement of the arms

2. Paddle swapping sides

To do this quickly, the best way is to change hands at the point the paddle crosses the centreline of the board with the top hand held high in preparation for the set-up phase

3. Paddle with exaggerated long strokes

With 5 second pauses to engage the core: 5 strokes per side and then change sides. Paddle for 1km

4. Deep squat strokes

Ten per side for 0.5km – great to practise paddling into the wind!

5. Paddle in surf stance

With feet across the centreline, one behind the other and in a wide stance. Practise regularly and in increasingly rougher conditions

6. Practise the catch

Stab the water and return to the set-up position – top hand high

MAKING PROGRESS WITH YOUR TECHNIQUE

A change in technique normally leads to a temporary drop in performance in any sport. So if you do make changes, you need to be aware of this. In fact, it can sometimes take some time for the muscular motor systems to catch up with the new movements. Your muscular systems and the fascial connections all take time to adapt.

During this time, practise patiently, deliberately with the confidence that the efforts will pay off.

How will you know when things are working?

- **Feeling:** you may feel faster, more powerful, more natural
- **Speed:** you may see it in terms of faster speeds
- **Economy:** you may find that you are far more capable of travelling at the same speed at lower heart rates for a longer time

Make sure that you are clear about why you are changing your technique before making the

	Perth and Kinross SUP			
Lap	Time	Distance km	Avg Pace min/km	
1	3:15.1	0.50	6:30	
2	3:11.0	0.50	6:22	
3	3:09.3	0.50	6:19	
4	3:11.6	0.50	6:23	
5	3:26.3	0.50	6:53	
6	3:17.0	0.50	6:34	
7	3:15.1	0.50	6:30	

An invaluable aid to evaluating your performance

changes. Otherwise, you will have no point of reference to map your progress.

The use of a GPS watch is invaluable in judging improvement. These devices provide feedback on the metrics that inform you on performance, such as heart rate, speed, stroke frequency and distance paddled. Anyone looking to improve should invest in one. We will look into these devices in more detail in the equipment section (Chapter 7).

SUMMARY

Unless you are a top pro, the chances are that your technique can be improved. There is no ideal paddle stroke, but committing to certain principles will help you paddle better. Effective force is gained by using the entire body in a coordinated manner.

You might like to use the dartboard below to identify the elements in your stroke that need attention. Then consider what actions you will take to improve the weaker aspects of your stroke.

Visualise what you want to achieve and recognise that power generation has phases.

Develop your bodily awareness and learn to switch on the power in different muscle groups at will.

Use the principles of a good paddle stroke to develop several strokes that can be used in different situations – such as downwinding, into the wind, cruising and drafting.

Recognise that your physical capability is a potential barrier and enabler to adopting a better technique.

This is the area we look at in the Chapter 5.

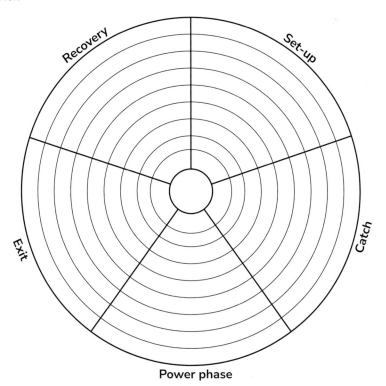

A paddle stroke dartboard
You can download this dartboard and blank ones from www.fernhurstbooks.com – search for 'Improving Your Stand Up Paddleboarding' and click on 'Additional Resources'

CHAPTER 4

IMPROVE YOUR SKILLS

Developing SUP skills is an enjoyable physical and mental challenge. The journey to mastery requires practice, patience and focus. Here we focus on seven skills that you can work on:

- The step back turn
- Changing paddle sides
- Drafting
- Downwinding
- Into the wind
- Into and out of waves
- Handling rebounds

THE STEP BACK TURN

What Is It?

The step back turn is a way of turning quickly.

Step onto the board's tail to lift the nose out of the water, then use a combination of paddle strokes to spin the board around.

Why Do It?

The step back turn is used in racing to navigate buoys. It is also advantageous when trying to catch waves. Even if you never do either, mastering this turn can be a personal challenge. It is an excellent test of balance, technique and athleticism. A feeling of warm satisfaction hits you when you do a fast, smooth turn in challenging conditions.

It involves fundamental movements and strokes that can be used in other situations. For example, the ability to freely move your feet up and down is essential when surfing or downwinding. Standing on the back of the board confidently is important when you are paddling back to the beach in an onshore break.

There is no one way of doing a step back turn. You need to find the works best for you.

Most people have a preferred stance – that is, you have a preferred leading foot along the board's centreline when going into surf stance. Goofy is right foot forward, and regular is left forward. Some people don't have a preferred foot.

An **open side turn** is where you paddle on the same side as your leading foot. In a **closed side turn**, your paddle side is opposite your lead foot. An open side turn feels more 'stable' than a closed side and can be completed in a few powerful broad strokes. A closed side turn generally uses smaller, faster strokes (as it is more difficult to gain power in this position).

Open Side Turn

To do a step back turn on the open side, you need to go through a number of phases:

1. Pick a target around which you are going to turn. A buoy is best, but pick a point in the water ahead of you if there are no buoys in the vicinity.
2. Build speed to the buoy. Speed provides stability – especially on a narrow board.
3. Visualise initiating the turn when the board is halfway past the buoy.
4. Before arriving at the buoy, prepare to move your feet. Approaching on the left-hand side of the buoy, your right foot will be the lead foot. Move the right foot to lie 90 degrees across the centreline when a board's length from the buoy. The left foot goes to a wide stance distance behind the right along the centreline.
5. Then step back by taking your right foot to your left and then your left back another big step. This should get your back foot onto the rear deck pad of a race board. (It might not, to start with, as your steps are likely to be less ambitious.) The key is that the back foot is sufficiently far back to lift the nose of the board out of the water. This makes the board easier to swing around in the opposite direction.
6. Use the paddle throughout. Keep it in the water bracing your movement. Perform one or two broad sweep strokes once the back foot is planted on the rear deck pad. The board should spin on the tail. If it doesn't, you have not gone far enough back.
7. Once the board has spun and the front is facing the desired direction, you need to get

your feet back to the middle of the board and 'paddle ready'. Do this by retracing your steps along the board's centreline while keeping the paddle trailing in the water for extra stability. With practice, you will find your feet moving quicker through this process.

Open Side Turn

Build up speed

Go into surf stance (lead foot on opposite side to paddle)

Step feet back

Paddle stroke deep to brace and turn

Lift nose by shifting weight to back foot

Use hips and sweep

If necessary use weight on front foot to keep stability

Sweep and control board with front foot weight

One final stroke

Brace if necessary as you move feet forward

Feet to parallel

Switch on the power

Other Important Factors

The legs must be bent and strong, and you should feel the sensation of a squat. You might find it helpful to stick your bum out. Keep your head reasonably high and constantly over the board's centreline. You can use your hips to resist the sweep stroke to get extra turning action.

Closed Side Turn

If you have a preferred stance, you will want to keep the same foot forward on both turns. Therefore, you will need to move your feet similarly to the open side turn, but the paddle is on the opposite side as you come to the buoy. It is more challenging to get a powerful stroke on this side. It is also more unstable. You will probably find yourself performing quicker, shorter strokes. Placement of the blade in the best location to pull the board round is essential. Most paddlers take a quick stroke on the opposite side to start the momentum of the turn.

Build speed

Adopt surf stance

Paddle on same side as lead foot

Start with small strokes

Brace if necessary!

Keep head central, nose lifts

Keep low and stable

Sweep strokes are shorter and quicker than open side

Nose is out of the water until complete

Variations On The Theme
Stepping Back
Rather than a 1-2 motion where the front foot steps back to the back foot and then the back foot moves back, in this variation, the front foot bypasses the back foot to become the back foot. This scissor movement is quicker and very slick, but needs practice.

Stepping Forwards
As you get more confident on the board, once the turn is completed, you can jump forwards to get into your paddling position at the front faster.

Changing The Top Hands Of The Paddle
You can use reverse paddle strokes on your open side by swapping the top hand for a closed side turn. This actually works really well.

A step back turn around a buoy

CHANGING PADDLE SIDES

A fast change of paddle sides can influence your stroke rate, whether you remain in the draft and even the result of a race. A poor switch of sides can cost a stroke and four changes of side per minute mean 4 strokes lost per minute. If each stroke represents a distance of 2.5m, you are losing 10m a minute through poor change-over technique. The switch of sides is worth practising!

The paddle switch should take place as the paddle moves over the board's centreline. At this point, the top hand comes off and goes into the lower position. The bottom hand then slides up to the top. The paddle should be in a position where you are ready to spear it into the water for the next catch without feeling like the rhythm is broken. Simple right? It's not easy.

Practise taking 3 strokes on each side before changing sides in a 15-minute segment of your training time. Get the conscious mind programmed, and the unconscious will eventually take over.

Changing paddle sides: Note that this takes place across the width of the board. This enables the paddler to change seamlessly without missing a stroke.

Blade comes out

Top hand releases

Top hand adopts bottom hand position

Previous bottom hand slides up the shaft

Now in the set-up position on the opposite side to where they started

Make next stroke

DRAFTING

What Is Drafting?

When the board glides through the water it creates a 'wake'. This wake varies depending on the shape of the board and, in particular, the tail. It is quite often seen as a set of triangular-shaped waves that radiate from the front of the board all the way to the tail edge. This wake is called the 'draft' of the board.

The side and tail of the board create waves that can be used for drafting

A paddler following can use this wake to great advantage. Locate your board approximately 0.3 to 0.5m away from the board in front and the draft will reduce the amount of effort required to maintain the same speed as the paddler in front. There is some experimentation to find the sweet spot, but once you find it, it is very noticeable.

A second location to draft is at the side of the board in front, as the wave here can be used to draft in its own right, or as a way of drifting into the draft at the tail. Maintaining your board in this sweet spot at the side requires more skill, but it's good fun.

Draft trains can range from two boards to twenty or more!

Drafting at the side requires more skill but is great fun

65

Why Draft?

If you intend to race, drafting is an essential skill. If you are a social paddler or tourer, you might wonder why you would ever bother. But it is still a skill that social paddlers would benefit from.

Why?

■ It is enjoyable. You feel like you are part of a larger unit – a single mass of paddlers. Each person has a role in keeping the integrity of the whole – whether leading or following.

■ It develops your paddling skills. It's a different challenge to paddling on your own. You mirror the person in front, observe their strokes, and predict where they are going while always being aware of the water around you.

■ It is a strangely hypnotic experience. After a while, you might find yourself becoming resonant with everyone else. Your stroke matches others, and you fall into an altered state of consciousness. You feel like you could paddle forever.

■ It can collectively increase paddling range substantially. Drafting saves each paddler energy. This is estimated to be about 30 percent. If a group gets caught out and has to face a stiff headwind on a return, the ability to draft will help get everyone safely home.

■ It fosters cooperation. In the act of drafting, the lead paddler will alter after an agreed period, so everyone shares the load. Each paddler takes the responsibility of being both leader and follower.

Drafting is very similar to the way the peleton works in a bicycle race.

The Technique

You need to keep your board's nose approximately 0.5m from the back of the board in front. This distance depends on the wake you observe from the board in front. You are trying to 'mount' the little wave that comes off the back. You are also aiming to keep in the flat undisturbed water that the board leaves as it moves forwards. It's tempting to drop your head as you focus on the back of the board ahead, but resist this as it will compromise your stroke.

Try to copy the paddling side of the paddler ahead. When they change sides, you change. Maintain a similar rhythm. This will help you to match the behaviour of the board in front. Also, observe the water around you. If you don't, it's easy to get caught out by waves, fishing lines or speedboats. Look further ahead to the lead paddler. Watch how they are paddling and use them to predict direction and pace.

When you are leading, pick a spot ahead and try to keep a straight line to it. This will make it easier for the paddlers behind. Try to look back now and again to make sure your colleagues are still with you.

Drafting is easier on flat water in calm conditions and gets progressively more difficult as conditions deteriorate. Drafting downwind is not worthwhile as catching waves might easily take you into the back of someone else.

Drafting Strategies

We will look at drafting strategies in the race section (P113). If you want to maintain a draft in a non-race situation, then work together as a team. Allow the strongest paddler to take on the most work but support each other by taking turns at the head.

DOWNWINDING

Why Do It?

Downwinding is one of the most enjoyable and fascinating aspects of SUP. It is a blend of power, fitness, strategy, imagination and excitement. It can provide feelings of elation and frustration in equal measure.

The feeling of being in flow occurs when you are stretched almost to the limit of your abilities but still have control. The ability to rise to, and meet a difficult challenge creates positive emotions and feelings of self 'growth'. Downwinding can definitely promote these sensations.

Downwinding involves starting at one point and using the wind and waves to take you to another point. You can either paddle upwind to the starting point or coordinate transport to the start (upwind) and end (downwind) points. You can downwind a stretch of sea or lake / loch.

It is best to practise in moderate winds of 8 to 10 knots and small waves. Take time to read the difference between wind waves and sea waves (see P32). Practise timing your paddling to harness the energy of the waves and get a feel for moving around on the board. Do not try to go fast. Try to find the technique of catching bumps and linking them together. Depending on your abilities, this can take months or years before you progress to stronger winds and deeper swells. Don't be in an undue hurry because the difficulty factor increases severely as wind speed and wave size increase.

Reading The Wind & The Sea

We have already mentioned that there are different waves on the sea (P32). The waves (we generally experience) are created by the wind. (Yes, earthquakes create waves, but hopefully, we won't be downwinding on a tsunami!) Particles of water in the sea do not actually move forwards, they rotate in a circle. Waves are like the ripple you can create on bedsheets when you make the bed. You give the sheet a flick, and a wave travels along with it. The sheet has not moved forwards, and each part of the sheet has not moved forwards. But the wave appears to move along the sheet by the rising and falling of the sheet 'particles'. This is important to understand.

The distance over which the wind blows is called the fetch. The more fetch, the more influence the wind has on the sea. The wind compresses the sea creating energy that has to be released in the form of waves.

Weather apps such as Windy provide information that is very useful to assess the suitability of a downwinder.

- **Swell:** the distance between trough and peak; anything over one metre starts to become challenging
- **Period:** the time period between wave peaks
- **Windspeed:** the speed of the wind, which will be denoted with an average and a gust speed; winds over 20 knots become challenging; over 30 knots and going upwind will be difficult for most people; over 35 knots and few paddlers will cope

Geography, depth of water, the force of the wind, tide, currents and duration of wind all affect the character of the waves.

Catching a wave on a downwinder

Quite often, there may be two or more swell waves. They may come from different directions and might complicate your intended direction. The wind will create another set of waves. These 'wind' waves will be smaller and travel slower than the 'swell' waves and are the easiest to catch.

Never try to catch a wave directly along its direction. Offset your board to the wave at an angle. You will find yourself zig-zagging instead of going in a straight line, and you will ride the waves longer and more successfully.

When waves from different sources meet each other, it causes interference – which looks messy. These areas are best avoided, but paddle hard to avoid getting stuck in them if you do encounter them.

To make sense of water, you really need to take the time to watch it move and study the patterns that emerge.

This looks like a good day to go out on a downwinder.

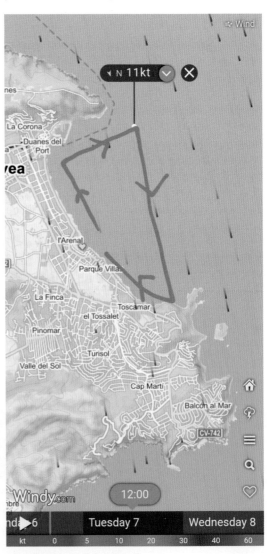

Here's a possible circuit

Planning A Downwind

Always try to downwind with others. If you start at point A and finish at B, you will need transport to point A and a vehicle waiting for you at point B. This will involve either a helpful friend or a downwinding companion. A reasonable distance for a downwinder is about 15km.

Alternatively you can incorporate a downwind into a circuit, by paddling upwind first (see route map opposite).

Use an app to gauge the wind and weather conditions and decide a date and time a few days ahead. Apps give you about five days of weather projections. They are not 100 percent accurate, so pick a date and time and then keep checking the app to ensure the weather is holding. You are looking at wind speed, wind direction, gust speeds and swell size / direction. A maximum of 15-knot wind and a moderate swell (0.4m) in the same direction will give you a nice downwind.

A strong swell at 90 degrees to the wind direction will make life difficult. The swell will constantly be trying to bump you off your intended course. Pick another day.

Equipment

If you generally don't wear a PFD (personal flotation device), wear one for downwinding. There is a chance of getting bumped from behind, falling backwards and banging your head on the board. Leashes stand more chance of being broken in wind and waves, increasing the possibility of losing the board in an incident. Yes, these situations are unlikely, but it's not worth taking the risk.

Ensure you have your standard kit, including a leash, waterproof pouch for car keys and mobile phone. Dress in a windproof jacket and wetsuit if the conditions require it. The wind driving through wet kit is unpleasant and cools the core temperature very quickly. Many tragic incidents at sea could have been prevented by wearing proper clothing. As you will probably be out in the open sea, make sure you can be seen by wearing bright fluorescent colours.

You must use a board that works for the conditions. It is possible to downwind on a flat water board, but you need to know what you are doing. Unless you are advanced, pick a wide board with some rocker (see P131). These will be more stable and easier to pick up the waves on. You need plenty of volume in the nose to help you pop up when you find yourself going from trough to crest.

Strategy & Technique

The strategy is to connect the waves from starting point to a finishing point, making the best use of conditions.

Catching little bumps: Little bumps and tufty wind waves require quick inputs of paddle power. Experiment with your cadence, but a short, deep, powerful, frequent stroke works well in these conditions. Work to keep the momentum high and try not to lose speed.

Bigger bumps: As wave size increases, they become less frequent. Consequently, you need to improve the timing and increase the power to catch them. You should aim to catch a wave with one stroke, then relax and let the wave take you. You can feel an approaching wave in your feet. The board tips forward as the wave develops, and it is at this point you need to switch the power on. Lower the bottom hand for extra power.

Watch the wave patterns ahead as a predictor for where and when you need to paddle. Use your peripheral vision and look on either side to see the imminent waves. If you are strong enough, paddle into the back of the wave ahead and wait for the wave behind to pick you up. If you are really strong, paddle through the bump in front to hitch a ride.

Bigger waves: Once waves are a certain size, they will be moving at a speed that most paddlers will find difficult to catch. You can waste a lot of energy trying to catch these, so focus on the smaller waves and play the law of averages.

Connor Baxter adopts a surf stance to catch the wave

Once on the wave he leans back

Watch for patterns: Aim to catch the second wave. The first wave tells you that a set is on its way. Once you have caught a wave, you will feel the board matching its speed. If the nose is burying in the water, you will need to step back to stop it from slowing you down and losing the wave. Experience will educate you on how far you need to step back.

Stop paddling when you are on a wave and stand relatively upright. If you continue to paddle, you might take yourself into the back of the wave in front. This will cause a complete loss of precious momentum. Stalling on a downwinder is frustrating.

You will get more comfortable moving around the board as you get better. You can use different stances to steer the board on the waves, and you can trim the board both back and forward to keep it flat to the water. Advanced paddlers sometimes adopt a surf stance in extreme conditions and literally surf the downwind.

Practice

Start slowly and deliberately. Educate yourself on wave patterns. Feel the way the board moves in different conditions. Practise long powerful strokes that engage the core interspersed with short punch strokes with high cadence. Go out with more experienced paddlers and watch how they go about things. Follow their routes and talk to them afterwards about what they saw and what they were trying to do.

Pro Tips

Paddle with a slight offset stance to better sense the board movements.

Use feet to steer the board: for example, steer to the left by putting more weight on the left and vice versa.

Downwinding requires strategy and strength

INTO THE WIND

Most people seem to hate paddling into the wind. But paddling into the wind is another fascinating challenge. It requires skill, technique, fitness and determination. Cast your mind back to the section on efficiency and the need to keep the board moving (P34). When going into a strong wind, this is essential.

Paddle directly into a strong wind and any deviation in direction is amplified. The turning force on the nose of the board can play havoc with direction, rhythm and mental wellbeing. Precision is vital. Your paddling must contain

minimal net turning force. This means you need to adopt an 'out-to-in' stroke (where your catch is some distance from the board edge and your exit takes place at the board edge – see P45), to constantly bring the board straight.

Because you are going into the wind, become lower to the water to be more streamlined.

Many paddlers adopt long fast strokes to keep the momentum. Short strokes can also be used, but they need to be deep and have high cadence.

The paddle recovery is crucial. It needs to

take the shortest route possible. Use your lower hand to actively throw the paddle forwards into the set-up phase. You should be aiming for 50-60 strokes per minute in a 20-knot wind. Keep the lower hand further down the shaft than normal to gain additional leverage, and adopt a low stance.

You also need to know your limit. Anything over 30 knots is a challenge for very good paddlers. Pick your challenges carefully. If the wind gets too strong, never be too proud not to resort to the knees paddling position.

The catch often suffers when going into the wind, so pay attention to keeping the reach long and the catch deep.

You really need high quality, consistent paddling to take a headwind on.

Paddling directly into a wind may be easier than paddling in a side wind, so it might be sensible to construct a route that does this.

Paddling into the wind

Adopt a low stance

Out-to-in stroke to keep board on track

Deep catch is essential

Paddle kept low on the recovery to minimise resistance from wind

INTO & OUT OF THE WAVES

Reading The Waves At The Beach

When waves get near the shore, they break. When and where this occurs depends on their size, the wind direction and the terrain under the sea. The shape of the beach will have a significant effect on the way the waves behave. A long, 'endless' beach will allow the sea to come into shore relatively undisturbed. The waves will be parallel to the shore.

In a cove beach, the sea is coming into an enclosed space. This causes interference wave patterns. The waves bounce off the walls creating rebounds that run across the primary wave. The central part of the wave will run to shore quicker than the sides. This creates a squeezing effect. A current will run up the sides and back out to sea. The water here will be more confused, but the resultant waves will be smaller, making it a more accessible place to enter from.

It is always prudent to study the terrain and the patterns before entering rougher waters. Look to time your entry into the water to correlate with a lull in the wave sets.

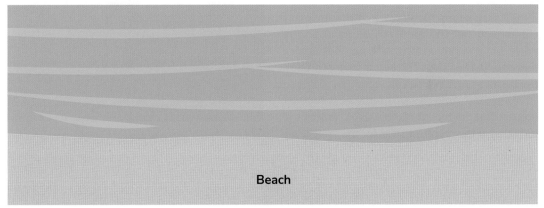

A long beach has no edges and undisturbed parallel waves

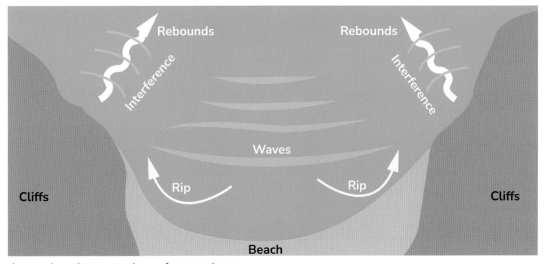

A cove beach creates lots of wave shapes

Into Waves

It can be a challenge to get out into the open sea (beyond the waves) when the waves are up. Indeed it can be quite intimidating.

You need good technique. You must keep the nose heading directly into the waves. Any other angle and the board will deflect, leaving the side of the board exposed to the wave's forces. If this happens, the board will immediately become difficult to control and, in all likelihood, you will be thrown off.

The nose will pitch into the sea as it hits an oncoming wave, so you need to lift it. You need to use the moves learnt in the step back turn to do this.

A metre before the wave, switch into a surf stance and get the nose up. As soon as the wave goes under, return to a parallel stance and paddle like crazy. The aim is to get through the break as fast as you can.

Adopt the same pattern for the next set until you are clear of the breaking waves. Watch the direction of the break and aim for the area away from where it originates.

If the waves are too powerful, it is no embarrassment to go out on your knees. Adopt the same strategy. Get the board heading nose-first into the waves. Sit slightly back from the centre so that the board nose can glide over the foamy water.

Get the nose up and paddle hard

Watch the way the waves break to decide the timing of your entry and the route you will take

Coming In With A Shore Break

You see walls of water rising and crashing down into an explosion of vapour ahead of you. The sound of breaking waves creates a feeling of panic and excitement. The first rule is to keep your calm. Take some deep breaths through the nose and take your time.

Pick the line back that you are confident with. Let the waves rise below you. When you get to the break, you need to think and be strong and powerful. If you can, look back and pick the wave. You will feel the angle of the board change as the wave rises. Start paddling hard. As the board's nose starts to go down, adopt the surf stance and step back to the board's tail. Keep paddling... keep the momentum.

As the wave breaks, make sure that your back foot is on the tail, and your front foot is on the centreline – a good squat distance ahead. Your legs should be bent, your head over the middle of the board and looking forwards. Take big powerful strokes. Shift your weight either onto the back foot or forward foot to keep it running flat.

Coming in on the break, start small and build confidence

In larger waves you will need to bend knees and get lower to ensure stability

SUP Surf

SUP surf provides all the fun of surfing without a lot of the effort. The ability to stand on a board and paddle through the waves is easier and drier! The SUP surfer can catch waves earlier and catch more of them. It is physically easier than surfing and makes catching waves accessible to many more people.

The art of surfing and much of SUP surf could occupy a book on its own and beyond what we can cover here. If you are interested in catching waves, here are some basic tips:

- Master the basics by only going out in small waves first.
- Practise interchanging a parallel and surf stance to lift the board over the waves.
- Practise turning the board by using a step back turn. This is relatively easy on a small board.
- Turn the board before the break and start paddling straight back. Feel the board dip as a wave comes in, immediately switch into surf stance to pick up the wave.
- Keep your head high and over the board while keeping your knees bent and bum sticking out.
- Use the paddle as a brace.
- Trim the board using your legs. Don't let the nose pitch into the water.

Once you have picked up the basics, progress into larger waves:

- Learn to use your front foot and back foot to control the board's speed. Weight on the front and the board usually accelerates; weight on the rear puts the brakes on.
- Learn to use your rear foot to direct the board. Leaning and moving your rear foot can get the board cutting back up the face of the wave. Things start to get exciting.
- Waves break to the left, right or all at the same time. Learn to set yourself up for each eventuality. Ideally, you want to ride along the face of a breaking wave ahead of the break. To start with, you might just be happy to surf straight back into the shore.
- Learn to relax during the inevitable wipe-outs. Develop an awareness of where your board is when it's not under your feet! When under the water, do not try to fight against the wave or grab your board via your leash. Keep calm and allow time for the wave to pass.
- Once you are dialled into catching waves 'straight', you can start to work on more elaborate moves that involve turning the board up and down the face of the wave. The cut-back turn is a classic sequence to learn, which will help you to stay on the wave longer.
- Other advanced skills you can learn include nose riding which involves walking up and down the front of the board while on a wave.

Two paddlers, one goofy (right foot forward) and one natural (left foot forward) handle a wave breaking to their right; in this instance, left foot forward will feel easier to most people

Weight is placed on front to accelerate the board

The hands cross over the board to use the paddle to steer the board

Nose riding involves walking to the nose of the board on a wave and requires skilled cross-stepping to maintain the trim

Be prepared for wipe-outs and keep relaxed

Cut Back Turn

Paddler looking up the wave. Note his weight is on the whole of the side rail. The paddle is extended for stability. Hard and committed lean to maintain speed.

Paddler is looking to where he will turn back down the wave. Shoulders and hips face the direction of travel

Using the momentum from the previous descent, the paddler has ridden back up the wave. He uses his paddle to dig in and is preparing the next turn.

The paddle is used to turn, but the waist and core are really working hard. His weight is on his back foot to change the board's direction. He has to be careful not to stall the board at this point.

Weight begins to shift to the front to start accelerating down the wave face.

Things to be aware of:

Getting caught inside: Caught inside means being too close to shore when a larger wave comes so that it breaks in front of or on you. If you cannot paddle over the wave, you're going to have to bail. If the area is clear, slip off to the side, duck and take the hit. Recover your board afterwards.

If the area around you isn't clear, turn your board to shore and belly ride it out of the impact zone into safety.

Etiquette and safety: Surf etiquette and rules of priority are long-standing and internationally recognised. SUP surfboards are quicker through the water, catch waves much earlier and are potentially much more hazardous than regular surfboards, so respect the surfers.

Don't paddle to the top of the line-up (i.e. the front of the queue!). There will be an existing and slightly fluid pecking order at all popular beaches. Take your time; if you are good enough, slowly work your way to where the best waves are breaking. Let everyone get used to your presence.

Right of way: The surfer deepest in the peak of the wave or closest to the breaking part of the wave has the right of way. This doesn't mean that you can spin around at the last moment inside someone who has clearly been waiting. This is called 'snaking' and isn't well received.

Dropping in: 'Dropping in' occurs when someone takes off on a wave already being ridden or when someone else has the right of way. Don't do it.

Paddling right of way: If you are in front of a wave that is being ridden and you will impede the surfer's ride, then you paddle towards the whitewater and take the hit. When paddling back out to the line-up in clear water, try to give the waves being ridden plenty of clearance by paddling wide.

Respect and awareness: Respect others, respect the beach and respect your level of experience and ability. Be aware of what's going on around you, the vibe in the water and any changes in the conditions or crowd.

Safety first: Always minimise the risk. It's just a wave, and there will always be another, so if there's any doubt, don't go. Always assist someone in difficulty.

HANDLING REBOUNDS

Reading Rebounds

Rebounds are intriguing. They occur when waves strike a resistant surface like a cliff or a harbour wall. A radiant wave is created that 'pings' out in the opposite direction to the wave that made it. These rebound waves actually contain a lot of energy. Consequently, you can catch and ride them. They can also cancel out the prevailing waves. On such occasions, you can observe the strange situation of flat water near cliffs while there is turbulence further out.

If you are paddling around a coastline, you need to watch out for these areas. They can be opportunities for easier paddling.

Rebound Paddling

Rebound paddling requires a similar technique to downwinding. You are looking to catch the rebound waves and ride them out away from their origin. They might not be easy to see, but they can be felt by the feet. When detected, switch on the power and feel the increase in speed. Once you have got one, ride the momentum of the following bumps. The speed you gain will help you cut through any other waves coming from other directions.

Catching rebounds can give you a ride

CHAPTER 5

IMPROVE YOUR PHYSICAL CAPABILITY

Why do people SUP? There will be many different reasons, but one common factor is that it makes them feel physically good. There is something invigorating about being in a natural environment and engaging in physical exercise. This feel-good factor extends beyond the duration of the activity. Scientists will rationalise these feelings as basic neurochemistry because exercise releases pleasurable substances like dopamine into the brain and body.

But there is something more than brain chemistry going on. The body and the mind come together and leave you with a sense of fulfillment. Exercise is both addictive and essential. We need it to express our human nature.

SUP is one of the most complete forms of exercise. It challenges the whole body, stimulates the mind and sharpens the senses.

SUP can be undertaken at various intensities. A gentle paddle on a local loch might hardly raise the heart rate; a 10km all-out race can leave even a top athlete utterly drained.

If you want to improve or just enjoy your paddling more, being 'SUP fit' will go a long way to enabling this. The good news for everyone is that, unlike many sports, there is no ideal physique that gives one athlete an advantage over another. Taller people can obtain more reach. Shorter people can attain higher cadence levels. Competitors, even at the highest level, vary in physique, proving the accessible nature of the activity.

However SUP is physically demanding, and an unprepared body and / or poor technique will leave you open to injury and lessen your enjoyment.

Ultimately most people SUP for enjoyment. The approach to SUP fitness should be designed to enhance this experience.

There are four areas of fitness that a paddler needs to develop:

1. Endurance
2. Power
3. Balance
4. Agility

Let's look in a bit more detail at the four foundations of SUP fitness.

1: ENDURANCE

What Is Endurance?

Endurance fitness is the essential facet of SUP fitness. Most people looking to improve at SUP need to address endurance as their priority.

Endurance is, literally, the ability to suffer. Humans are exceptionally well adapted to endurance activity. The human body has several unique features that allow it to endure prolonged exercise over long distances better than any other mammal.

In sports language, endurance concerns suffering over a certain distance while going at the fastest sustainable speed. The enemy of endurance is fatigue. Go beyond a certain level of intensity and fatigue quickly reduces performance. Endurance training is designed to improve the ability of an athlete to go as fast as possible over a certain distance.

Cardiovascular endurance relates to heart rates and breathing. It reflects how effective the heart is at delivering oxygen to muscles via red blood cells.

Muscular endurance concerns the ability to perform and sustain repeated load-bearing tasks – like thousands of paddle strokes per hour.

The capacity to endure has importance to all paddlers:

- If you enjoy touring, you want to be able to paddle a decent touring distance over a day
- If you do SUP surf, you want to be in the waves at full power the whole time
- If you SUP for fitness, you want to sustain your exercise sessions
- If you race, your success will be primarily determined by your endurance capabilities

The prevalent assumption that acts as the foundation for training is that endurance is improved by applying a 'load' and allowing the body to recover. The theory says that the body makes subsequent adaptations during the recovery phase that enables a person to handle more load in the future.

The theory appears to be valid, but anyone looking to get fitter should do so with patience, not haste. Overtraining can actually create the opposite effect to what you are looking for!

Turning Food Into Movement

Without going into pages of detail, the following factors are at play:

- Air sacs in the lungs (called alveoli) pull oxygen from each breath
- The heart pumps the resultant oxygen-rich blood to muscles
- Muscles convert chemical energy stored in the body (in the form of sugar or fat) into physical movement
- Fuel for energy can be obtained through eating fat or carbohydrates
- The power a body can generate depends on the amount of oxygen it can process
- At aerobic intensities, the body chooses which fuel to burn based on what is available (carbohydrates, fats, proteins)
- At anaerobic intensities, only glucose can be utilised

So, the things that anyone interested in performance needs to optimise are:

A. Oxygen intake
B. The volume of blood circulating
C. Metabolic processes
D. The profile of muscle fibres

A. Oxygen Intake

Breathing enables oxygen to enter the body. The nose is the organ that should be used as it enables the intricate functions of the body to work correctly. Many health problems stem from dysfunctional breathing.

There are significant benefits to breathing through your nose. It:

- Pre heats the air into the passageways reducing shock
- Filters the air before entering the lungs
- Gets oxygen deeper into the alveoli
- Develops nitrous oxide in the nasal cavity: this is a powerful antiviral and increases blood supply to cells
- Reduces feelings of stress in the central nervous system

Conversely, mouth breathing:

- Activates stress receptors that trigger burning sugar, not fat
- Denies the influence of the calming oxygen-rich lower lobes
- Compromises waste removal through the lower lung
- Promotes neck and shoulder tightness due to excessive upper chest breathing

The way you breathe has a significant influence on oxygen uptake. Frequent shallow breathing can deplete oxygen levels rather than increase them.

All exercise should be undertaken with nasal breathing. You should aim to take long breaths both in and out. Look to breathe no more than 15-20 times per minute. This takes significant practice and focus. If your stroke rate is 45 strokes per minute, look to complete one breath cycle every three strokes. Be patient, start slowly, be deliberate and allow the results to follow over months rather than days.

Most people do not give their breathing conscious attention. In sport, many athletes breathe rapidly through their mouths in an attempt to maximise performance. This is sub-optimal and unhealthy. Nasal breathing is essential and beneficial to endurance.

B. Blood Circulation

Jim Fixx was a famous runner of the 1970s. He

wrote the bestseller, *The Complete Book Of Running*. His philosophy was mind over matter, and he committed to running 10 miles a day, every day, for the rest of his life. Some years later, while still in his mid-50s, he collapsed and died after his gruelling daily routine.

The idea that 'exercise is good for you' does not mean that more exercise is 'even better for you'!

The heart is far more intricate than a sophisticated pump and should be treated respectfully.

Your heart rate rises with intensity, and two threshold points are essential to be aware of when you are exercising.

Point 1: The Aerobic Threshold: The point where aerobic stress begins.

This is the point where any further level of intensity would prevent you from holding a conversation with someone else while nose breathing. This point is associated with a heart rate level called L2.

To find your aerobic threshold level

Go out on the water and paddle slowly for ten minutes to sense what is going on in your body. In particular, pay attention to your breathing and heart rate (not by looking at it – by feeling it). Slowly increase the intensity until you feel a 'catch' in your body. It is not an easy sensation to describe, but you will feel a switch at a certain level of exertion. At this point, you will probably not be able to hold a conversation evenly and with focus. This is your L2 heart rate. Play around for a further ten minutes to confirm the feeling, and then look at your GPS for the heart rate. This is the most important number for your training and general activity.

Point 2: The Lactate Threshold: The point where, during anaerobic exercise, perfomance becomes difficult to maintain or no longer possible due to the lactate production within the muscles.

Most people can only withstand the sensations associated with anaerobic exercise for a few minutes. Experienced athletes can last longer, maybe up to an hour. This point is called the lactate threshold. It occurs at the L4 heart rate level.

Heart Rate Levels
Most GPS devices have heart rate monitors on them. These are very useful to provide real-time information on your heart rate.

On the Garmin, five levels describe the different physical states of the athlete by heart rate.

Level (L)	Heart rate as a % of max	Perceived exertion
1	50-60	Relaxed easy
2	60-70	Comfortable conversation possible
3	70-80	Moderate pace but conversation difficult to hold
4	80-90	Fast pace, uncomfortable forceful breathing
5	90-100	Sprint pace, unsustainable for more than a few minutes

Note that the percentages are notional or averages and may not reflect your personal profile accurately

Aerobic Training

All paddlers looking to improve SUP fitness should work on their aerobic base. This can only be done by paddling most of the time in the L2 region. For many sportspeople, this appears counter-intuitive. They believe in the 'no pain, no gain' school and are keen to increase intensity at every opportunity. However, good things come to those who wait. You cannot shortcut the building of aerobic capacity.

If you ignore a slow, methodical approach, you risk becoming 'aerobically deficient'. This occurs when athletes train too much at high intensities (L4 and L5). A consequence of this is that their heart rate immediately jumps to a high beats per minute even during moderate exercise intensity. This is not healthy and places unnecessary strain on the heart.

To build an aerobic base, spend 90 percent of your training time in L2. In order to develop anaerobic capacity, spend the remaining 10 percent of time undertaking intervals in L4.

Anaerobic Training

Interval training was devised by Woldemar Gerschler in the 1930s. He found that the rest periods between intense exercise generated preferential changes in the heart muscle that improved its performance. An athlete could incorporate more intensity into a set training time by going fast, resting and then repeating than by just going fast non-stop!

Intervals can be used to build all-out anaerobic capacity or muscular endurance. Intervals should range from 30 seconds to a maximum of 8 minutes. For example, 30-second intervals would be used for developing maximum speed, while longer a interval would focus on endurance.

The key to successful intervals is to ensure that each set is completed at the required L4 intensity and that full recovery is achieved between intervals. Full recovery is a reduction in heart rate of at least 25bpm.

Most people do not need to perform more than one interval session a week to gain significant benefits. This is a far more effective and healthier method of creating adaptations in the heart muscles than overwhelming them with extended periods of intense stress.

C. Metabolic Flexibility

Conventional wisdom says that active sports-orientated people should be eating 60 percent of their food intake as carbohydrates. This convention has been strongly challenged over the last 20 years.

Carbohydrates are used as a form of fuel by the body as glucose, whereas fats are used to maintain structure and used as fuel. Fat consumption is critical for many tissues – for example, the brain is 60 percent fat.

The amount of glucose that our blood holds at any time is only about a teaspoon's worth. The body calls on insulin to strictly regulate glucose levels as elevated levels are harmful to

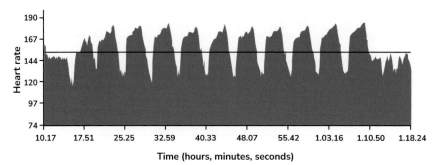

Almost perfect interval session: progressively more intense, good recovery in the intervals and evenly timed, with recovery afterwards

our health. The body stores a limited amount of glucose (as glycogen) in the liver (400 calories worth) and in the muscles (1,600 calories). Undertaking a long-distance event and relying solely on carbohydrates can become a logistical challenge because you need to carefully balance the calories in and out.

The body stores over 10,000 calories of fat. This is a plentiful energy store that could fuel an athlete over days of exertion. Metabolically flexible people have the ability to burn fat in preference to carbohydrates. As a consequence, concerns over precise refuelling requirements become redundant.

Gaining metabolic flexibility requires reducing carbohydrate intake and increasing fat intake in general eating. This can be done by removing sugar and processed foods, cereals and most fruit from the diet. Lost calories from carbohydrates should be replaced with unsaturated fats – such as those derived from eggs, unprocessed meat, nuts, avocados and seeds. All commercial energy drinks should be avoided. The transition can be done incrementally to avoid the feeling of 'hitting the wall' that carbohydrate-dependent athletes often encounter. Over time your body will adapt to burning fat first rather than carbohydrates, leaving you in a much more resourceful place to pursue endurance activities.

Extensive L2 training fits perfectly with a more fat-oriented diet, as training at L2 you should be exclusively burning fat. The benefit of being fat adapted is that your glucose stores can then be reserved exclusively for higher intensities – for example, the sprint finishes when racing or hard paddling into the wind if you need to when touring.

Protein is essential for muscular recovery and development, and everyday functions of the body. Protein consumption and absorption is dependent on an individual's age, weight and exercise level. Younger athletes can get results from taking in 20g after exercise. An older person, whose body does not synthesise

protein as efficiently, needs to take 40g.

Protein is best consumed immediately after exercise. There is approximately 6g of protein in an egg – so the amounts required are sizable. Protein supplements are convenient for this reason. Protein plays a major role in recovery after physical exercise – so do not disregard the need to supplement if you are active in the water!

Sufficient hydration is critical for endurance performance. Lose more than 2 percent of your body weight in fluids, and performance will be compromised by up to 35 percent. Recommendations on hydration from sports scientists are as follows:

- 600ml (water or electrolyte) 2 hours before exercise
- 300ml 20 minutes before exercise
- 300ml every 20 minutes during exercise

It is possible to drink too much water as well as too little. It is also possible to train your body to sustain exercise with reduced hydration levels. In fact, drinking electrolyte drinks (without glucose) is a more effective pre-workout option. Furthermore, using sodium bicarbonate or sodium citrate may help the body deal better with handling the lactate threshold.

D. Muscle Fibre Profile

Not all muscles are the same. There are generally recognised to be three types:

- **Slow-twitch muscle fibres:** the main sustainers of endurance; these muscles operate 'aerobically'
- **Fast-twitch muscle fibres:** the main sustainers for short bursts of energy such as sprinting, jumping and lifting heavy weights; these muscles work 'anaerobically'
- **Hybrid muscle fibres:** can adapt to either fast or slow-twitch functions – these muscles rebalance their function depending on the loading patterns they habitually experience

A marathon runner's physique is quite different from a 100m sprinter. Both athletes run, but the physical demands of each distance are quite different. The 100m sprint requires explosive movement over a very short duration. A 100m sprinter will have a high proportion of fast-twitch muscle. A long-distance runner carries less pronounced musculature, as their bodies are predominantly slow-twitch.

On average, a SUP paddler's physique will fall somewhere in between these extremes. A paddler requires more power interventions than a marathon runner and far more endurance than a 100m sprinter. SUP involves the whole body to a much higher degree than running.

Look at famous male SUP athletes, and most are powerfully built with highly muscled shoulders, lats, arms and core. There are exceptions like Bruno Hasulyo, whose wiry spring-like physique is reflected in his high cadence technique. Female SUPers tend to rely less on upper body strength than their male compatriots and use their lower body strength to drive the board forward.

Your existing fibre profile will influence the characteristics of your technique. If you need to adapt it, you need to develop your twitch profile accordingly. This is often easier to do off water through plyometric and strength-based exercises than trying to do this on the water. We suggest some exercises you can do in the section covering power below.

2. POWER

The application of power causes us to move. The more power you can generate, the faster you can go. Power must be transferred from the body to the paddle via the stroke. The quality of the stroke determines how well we use the power generated. But power itself stems from a combination of strength and speed. Strength is the ability to create force, and speed is how quickly the force can be applied. This is why people can be less 'strong' (in terms of

deadlifting) than someone else, but be more 'powerful' than them.

Power stems from:

A. Strength
B. Speed
C. Highly adapted fascial networks
D. Well-conditioned soft tissue
E. Sound biomechanical application

A. Strength

To build strength, you need to load your body. This can be achieved through weights or other forms of resistance, including body weight or resistance bands. For an activity such as SUP, you need to recruit strength from all parts of the body – at the same time. Therefore, range of movement exercises that build intramuscular motor units are more effective than isolated movements. For example, an air squat (which involves both the lower and upper body over a movement cycle) would be more beneficial than a bicep curl (a singular muscle movement).

Strength training will help a paddler to gain more stability, more power and greater muscular endurance. Strength training can be undertaken with or without weights.

Repetition and speed of the movement affect how the body responds to load:

- **All-out strength** is built from near-maximal loading and low repetitions
- **Endurance strength** is built from faster movements with lighter resistance and more repetition

All-Out Strength Exercises

To make adaptive changes to your body, it is recommended to undertake two resistance training sessions per week. Maintaining form in exercise movement is more important than the number of repetitions. Care must be taken not to overload joints and the central nervous system. Strength training should follow on from fascia training for reasons that we explain later. Rest, recovery and nutrition are vital components of any strength-building approach.

All-out strength exercises

Kettlebell exercise: for back and triceps. Using hips as a lever, bend over resting one hand on the wall for stability. Maintain a straight back and lift opposing elbow back (only the arm with the weight should be moving; do not allow the back, legs or opposing arm to move). Repeat 10-20 times each side depending on weight used.

Curl and press: for arms and shoulders. 1. Stand with feet shoulder-width apart, back straight, shoulders rolled back and arms hanging naturally down by side. 2. Bring the weight from hip to shoulder, by keeping elbows tucked in using elbows as a lever – this is the bicep curl. 3. Then shoulder press the weight above the head (keeping weight in line with body, palm facing forward or inward, in one swift motion). Repeat 10-20 times each side depending on weight used.

Endurance Strength Exercises

These are the critical exercises for anyone looking to build their SUP fitness. They can be done without equipment and take minimal time. These exercises can be coordinated into a 15-minute set. Undertake each exercise for 30 to 60 seconds and take 20 seconds rest between exercises. These movements will transform your ability to generate power. You will feel younger, springier and fitter. There are many fitness apps available that offer timed structured sessions that you can follow easily and conveniently. These apps act as personal trainers!

Endurance strength exercises

Air squat and jump: for legs and plyometrics. Keeping feet planted flat on the ground and back straight, squat down (use the arms to balance by holding straight out in front), then jump and land with bent knees (to prevent injury). Repeat 20 times.

Reverse lunge: for legs and core balance. Keeping one foot planted flat, step opposing leg back creating a right angle with each knee, until rear knee almost touches the ground. (Keep back straight and hold arms out to the side for balance). Repeat with other leg. Repeat 15 times each side.

Mountain climber. Keeping arms straight and hands underneath shoulders, alternate bringing each knee to the chest (or as close as possible). Keep supporting leg as straight as possible for support and injury prevention. Repeat 20 times each side.

Endurance strength exercises (continued)

Walk out to the plank. Resting body weight on slightly bent legs (1), bend over from standing, keeping lower and mid back straight. Walk hands forward (2) out to plank position (3) (where hands are underneath shoulders). Walk hands back (4) then return to upright standing position (5 & 6). Repeat 10 times.

Kettlebell swing. Hold the kettlebell with both hands (palms facing self), in a wide leg stance. Swing the weight from between legs (using a thrust of the hips from the glute muscles), up to around shoulder height. Allow weight to swing back down with straight arms, ensuring the back is kept straight throughout whole movement. Repeat 10-20 times.

Endurance strength exercises (continued)

Burpee. From standing position, drop into a plank position by pushing the legs backwards and taking the weight on your arms and shoulders. From this position bring the feet to the hands and jump explosively and vertically. Repeat 10 times.

B. Speed

As we have already stated, power is strength combined with speed. Ensuring your body can move with speed is necessary to produce power. Speed of movement depends on having a good range of motion and an elastic, responsive body. To gain power requires training the neuromuscular system to move explosively. This is best done by doing plyometric exercises, that incorporate a range of jumps.

Plyometric exercises
Squat jumps, box jumps, standing long jump, standing high jump

Squat jump. Legs shoulder width apart. Lower into squat and then jump vertically using arms to propel you into the air. Repeat up to 20 times.

The beauty of plyometrics is that you can work the entire body very effectively and quickly. You don't need any equipment, and the exercises can be done anywhere. Plyometric exercises develop a magical substance in everyone's body – fascia.

C. Fascial Networks

Our bodies are wonders of nature. They are a complex, integrated system that operates as a whole. They consists of bones, muscles, ligaments, tendons and a neurotransmission system. The muscles tend to get all the attention when considering strength and power. There are over 600 muscles in the human body. Most of them extend and contract. When they contract, they take on load. When they extend, they allow another muscle to contract. Muscle motor units thread muscle activity together to create more extensive strength areas than just the muscle itself.

But another part of our anatomy integrates these familiar parts: the fascia. In the past, the fascia system was largely ignored by the field of biomechanics because it would virtually disappear when dissecting a body! Muscles cannot function effectively without fascia. Fascia conducts muscular strength all around the body.

The skeletal system is seen as the prominent structural element of the body. The skeletal system has no structural integrity without the fascia binding it together.

Fascia is a thin continuous solid mesh of fibrous connective tissue that provides support and protection for muscle and bones. These tissue fibres are made up of collagen and elastin fibres. These are suspended in a fluid called the 'ground' substance. Fascia has a tensile strength of 900kg, and it envelops the entire body from the tips of the toes to the top of the head.

This network of tissue is arranged in a spring-like coil pattern around the legs and waist and then wraps its way up opposite sides of the upper body. Think of it as a super-intelligent, highly adaptable wonder suit that provides your body with elastic energy, structural integrity under load and essential flexibility.

There are several prominent 'grids' of fascia wrapped around the body to support planes of movement. They enable the body to bend forwards and backwards, and tilt side to side.

The fascia has varying consistencies within the body: in some areas it mimics that of liquid (whilst still remaining fibrous) in others it is much more solid and fibrous. The fascia allows a cricketer to catch a ball travelling at 100 miles an hour without breaking their hand. As the ball impacts the hand, the energy is dissipated throughout the fascia network. Without this response to load, the cricketer's hand would be badly damaged. It is similar every time you jump or skip. Your fascia is constantly adapting, absorbing, springing according to how you move and hold yourself.

Fascial tissue has more proprioceptive sensors than any other organ in the body. Look after your fascia, and your sense of balance will improve,

Experiments have shown that the strength of the muscular system is increased by at least 40 percent through the engagement of the fascia system. Because this material wraps itself around every part of the body in a structural mesh, it acts together as one unit. Therefore, it can conduct strength from one part of your body to another location. It is highly 'trainable' and consequently can be used as a game-changer in developing physical performance.

Many power and speed techniques focus on building and conditioning muscle. Muscle is easy to train and sense. Fascia takes longer to programme, but athletes should focus on it before embarking on muscle-related strength training. A well-conditioned fascial system will support advances in muscular strength. Attempting to build muscle mass without investment in your fascia will lead to soft tissue injury.

Fascia training initially needs a slow and deliberate approach to encourage proper form. Speed can be increased as the tissues and the nervous system adapt to the movements and load. (This is another reason to focus training in the L2 zone – see P83 – as this encourages slower, deliberate practice of movement.)

Remember our brief description of Bruce Lee in Chapter 2 (P36). His secret was the way he could connect up all the power from his individual body parts and channel it into his fist, using fascia as the conduit.

You can become a 'SUP black belt' and generate more power, gain more nimbleness and enjoy more stability by training your fascia. It might take 6 to 12 months to develop and to do this, you will need to undertake regular exercises and look after your fascia with massage and stretching. It will be time well spent. You will feel younger, fitter, stronger and more able to tap into power. You will improve your elasticity and generate free energy in your stroke as a consequence.

Exercises to develop the fascia

As well as plyometric exercises, activities such as yoga, pilates and martial arts offer excellent opportunities to develop your fascia.

Pilates and yoga can develop fascial strength

The Sun Salutation (taken from yoga – see P122) is a fantastic set of moves, combined with breathing, to stimulate the fascial networks.

D. Soft Tissue

There are a number of ways you can ensure your soft tissue is well conditioned, including activation and dynamic stretching which both stimulate the muscular system and help build elastic energy.

Activation: Through underuse, muscles can condition themselves to stop activating. The body is resourceful and other muscles will take on the load. This will cause pain and injury when they become overworked and eventually break down.

For example, extended periods of sitting can switch off the glutes. The glutes are some of the most powerful muscles in the body, and your core strength is compromised if they are not engaged (e.g. in activities such as lifting). Back injuries often result from this. People believe that they have weak backs when it is really the case that muscle groups have deactivated. You can discover deactivated areas when you undertake plyometric exercises (see P91). For example, if you struggle to squat it is probably because your glutes are not switching on.

You can switch muscle groups back on by consciously contracting them. This is called activation.

Dynamic stretching: A fantastic way to prepare areas of the body for exercise. It involves undertaking a number of movements to stimulate muscle groups.

Activation and dynamic stretching exercises

Simple pre-exercise movements can activate and prepare the muscles for activity.
For example, our recommended pre paddle movements are:

Shoulder circles: rotate both arms together, but in opposite directions

Hip openers: with legs apart, lean one side, then the other

Activation and dynamic stretching exercises (continued)

Dynamic chest stretches: move the arms from outstretched in front of you to the side

Side tilts: raise one arm & lean over; repeat the other side. Use your core and don't overstretch your back.

 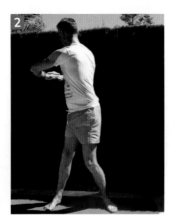 

Back twists: with your arms held together out in front, twist round each way

Static Stretching: Static stretching takes place where poses are held for more extended periods – usually 15 seconds or more. Static stretches should be done in the evening or on days when no exercise is planned. Static stretching can initially weaken the system leaving you susceptible to injury, and should never be done pre-exercise.

Undertake static stretching over a period of a month and you will see increases in your range of movement. This will translate into benefits in gains of power and stability.

Static stretching has been found to be most beneficial when coordinated with breathing techniques. Breathe in through the nose for a count of four and out through the mouth for a count of eight and you will enjoy even greater progress.

Static stretching exercises

The hamstring stretch is essential to develop improved balance. From laying down, raise one leg up. Feel the stretch from the buttocks to the ankles. Breathe in through the nose and out through the mouth and hold for 5 minutes. You can use a band around the foot.

Shoulders are highly vulnerable to injury in paddling. This shoulder stretch will develop and maintain shoulder mobility. Use your paddle to hold this stretch for 5 minutes with the same breathing pattern as for the hamstring stretch.

Flossing and foam rolling: Flossing and foam rolling are forms of myofascial release to stimulate healing and alleviate pain. Flossing involves using a large rubber 'band' to wrap around affected areas like a tourniquet. This increases blood flow to that area, accelerating healing and recovery. Foam rolling uses pressure in local areas through a 'roller' to repair and change the composition of the fascia.

Flossing the elbow

Foam rolling the glute

Massage: Massage is a technique of using hand or artificial devices to stimulate blood flow to the muscle. Doing so speeds up the delivery of nutrients to the affected area and the removal of metabolic waste. Massage can also reduce nerve compression and relax muscle tissue. A consequence of this is a reduction in pain and spasms.

Massaging with spikey balls

You can undertake all of these soft tissue practices on yourself. For specific areas of concern, you can reference YouTube for guidance in particular detailed movements.

The more you become in tune with your body, the better you will identify your own ways of alleviating pain and relaxing your body.

E. Sound Biomechanics

The body moves in three planes under a complex architecture of soft tissue and sophisticated joints. You need to be strong in all three planes, as any weakness will be revealed by intense or prolonged exercise.

If you suffer pain after paddling, do not ignore it.

Soft tissue issues occur when the body cannot disperse the load effectively and the part doing the most work fatigues. The cause is usually because another part of the body is not doing its part. For example, hip pain can be caused by irregularities or injuries in the ankle: the lower leg's range of motion can become compromised, creating eccentric loading and an overload to the hips.

You need to understand the source of pain. You also need to address the pain and ensure it does not occur again. Soft tissue injury responds well to attention through massage, rest, stretching and flossing. But if you ignore the pain, it can 'progress' to become chronic.

Chronic pain is debilitating but can become 'accepted' as the 'price to pay' to do what you enjoy doing. Never accept this because your body will compromise movement until you have harder-to-fix problems that affect joints and bone.

It pays to listen to your body early and take appropriate action. You need to become your own 'pain detective' because no one knows your body as you do.

Paddlers do seem to suffer particular injuries. These are often located at joints. By implication, joints are points of mobility. This makes them vulnerable to stress from eccentric loads.

Shoulder injuries: The shoulder is a very complex joint. With complexity comes vulnerability. The shoulder joint must be looked after because it is difficult to repair and difficult to live with if painful! Shoulder injuries are usually a result of a technique that does not suit the paddler. They either need to strengthen the

The elbow can be one of the first joints to complain about poor technique: these photos show different elbow positions: higher and lower

area in question or shift the power generation closer to the core. Sometimes a simple change in blade size can work. Experimenting with the top hand and top elbow position can identify the cause and how to avoid it.

Elbow injuries: The elbow is another complex joint. The musculature surrounding the elbow is not particularly strong. Compare the fibrous, dense, springy mass of your glute with the refined lightweight material of your forearms. The elbow has a motorway of nerves and tendons running around it from the hand back to the brain. Golfer's elbow and tennis elbow are common injuries. The problem with both of these afflictions is that they can be very difficult to shake off. So they are best avoided. There can be various reasons why pain appears in this area – technique, old injuries, weak wrists or weak triceps, to name four. Your own detective work is the only route to find the solution.

In his book *Waterman 2.0*, Kelly Starrett provides a thorough guide to maintaining paddle fitness. He claims that the top paddle hand elbow must be parallel to or above the top hand to avoid injury. This is not universally agreed, as other paddlers claim that the elbow is better kept lower, vertically below the hand.

What should you do? Experiment and possibly vary the position so as not to fatigue it in any position. Furthermore, pay special attention to this area in your stretching and foam rolling practice.

Neck injuries: The neck can be injured through poor technique. Many people will push their heads forward and hold it stiffly when under stress. This response is linked to the 'fight or flight' behaviour. These people are preparing to fight. Having such a position for any period of time places strain on the neck and back. This can be addressed by making sure you keep good postural angles at all times.

Keep the neck in alignment with your back to avoid strain as in photo 2, not as in photos 1 or 3

3: BALANCE

We looked briefly at the subject of balance when looking at efficiency. There are three systems used in the body to enable the sense of balance:

- **Proprioception:** the sensors within your body that inform you where you are in space and the appropriate strength response, such as gripping a paddle
- **The visual sense:** the use of your eyes to reference your body within the external environment
- **The vestibular sense:** via the fluids in the ear canal: a kind of spirit level of the inner ear

Most people are highly reliant on their sense of sight. Look at the difference of the average timings standing on one leg between eyes open versus eyes closed for the following age groups:

Age	Eyes open	Eyes closed
Under 40	45 seconds	15 seconds
41-50	42 seconds	13 seconds
51-60	41 seconds	8 seconds
61-70	32 seconds	4 seconds

Ways To Improve Balance

Given that your visual ability will probably be best developed, switch your attention to the other systems whenever you can. Balancing exercises where you close your eyes work well. To build your proprioception, you need to stimulate the appropriate sensors in your skin and fascia. Given that your feet are the only part of the body in contact with the board and have a disproportionate amount of nerve endings in them, they are an ideal place to start.

Ways to develop proprioception in your feet are:

- Walk around in bare feet
- Run barefooted in the sand
- Jump and run on the spot: this stimulates the fascia
- Use a spikey ball regularly to massage the base of your feet
- Regularly stretch and manipulate your feet to relax them and make them feel loved!

There are many other ways to improve balance, but the foundation is to have strong legs. A regimen of squats and jumps build the necessary strength. If you can't do 30 consecutive air squats and cannot hold a deep squat for a minute, you probably have work to do.

Bosu ball exercises

A Bosu balance ball is great to improve your balance. The exercises develop your spatial awareness and strengthen the ankle's small muscles, which are vital for balancing on a SUP board. Some exercises are listed below – depending on your current capability, start further down the list!

1. Stand on the flat side and practise different feet positions
2. Stand on the squidgy side and run on the spot
3. Stand one-legged on the flat side
4. Stand one-legged on the squidgy side
5. Do all the above with your eyes closed
6. Do a one-legged squat on either side of the Bosu ball

Stand on the flat side and practise different feet positions

Stand on the squidgy side and run on the spot

Stand one-legged on the squidgy side

4: AGILITY

Wikipedia defines agility as:

The ability to change the body's position efficiently and requires the integration of isolated movement skills using a combination of balance, coordination, speed, strength and endurance

Why Agility Is Important

Watch a pro handle rough surf with a race board and you will see how much they move up and down the board. They are constantly correcting and twisting their bodies to maintain direction and stability. They contort their bodies in all three planes of movement (side to side, backwards to forwards, up and down) with sudden powerful changes in direction. Agility is the key to this feat. As you improve as a paddler, you become more aware of the importance of being agile.

You need to be agile to get the best out of SUP surf or downwinding.

It is very noticeable how agility diminishes as people age. Older paddlers can retain strength and endurance well into their sixties, but their ability to dance on the board slows. The reason is not just genetic. As most people get older, they stop moving their bodies as dynamically as they did when they were younger.

Plyometric exercises are an excellent way to reinstate or preserve agility because they combine three important elements of agility: endurance, power and balance. These drills all work on quick changes of direction, rapid motor skills and the use of the whole body. If you feel a bit sluggish on your board, these will help.

Exercises To Improve Agility
Lateral (side-to-side) plyometric jumps

Create a line in front of you (using a rope or similar). You will jump forwards and laterally over the line and continue back and forth over the line for several jumps. Get into a squat, shift weight from heels to toes and jump. Pay attention to your landing and keep your shoulders and hips facing forward.

Lateral plyometric jumps; go into a squat and jump in a zig-zag pattern

Exercises To Improve Agility (continued)
Bosu ball lateral (side-to-side) jumping exercises

Starting on one side, step on ball with nearest foot (first foot)

Other foot follows

Both feet momentarily in contact with ball

First foot moves to other side and taps the ground

First foot returns to ball

Second foot taps ground, then repeat sequence twenty times building foot speed

GETTING SERIOUS: TRAINING FOR RESULTS

Training Plans

For many people the idea of creating a training plan to improve their SUP will seem excessive. However, for those who are keen to compete, developing a training plan will be a logical extension to the material we have already covered.

The plan should reflect your major goals or ambitions for the year. It should contain a logical build-up and address the areas you believe are most pertinent to your SUP fitness.

Why would you consider preparing a training plan if you are not competing?

There are several reasons why it might still be worthwhile to write down your fitness goals for the year ahead:

- It helps you to reflect on your current abilities
- It helps you create ambition for how you would like to progress
- It provides some structure to your weekly activities that will facilitate progress
- It will result in a feeling of greater health and fitness at the end of the season

Training plans are tailored to individuals based on their current fitness and abilities and their goals for the coming season. Here are some general ideas to help with your training plan:

Set the goals for the forthcoming season: This could be participating in certain events, going a certain distance or perfecting a skill. Be careful not to put too much outcome-focused pressure by saying 'to win' or 'to beat'. SUP mastery is about doing the best you can regardless of the result.

Work back from the critical events: This is your timeline of preparation. Allow a week before the event of light training, two weeks before that for a tapering off of intensity.

- It seems generally accepted to work training in 4-week blocks. In each 4-week block, the intensity of week 2 is higher than week 1,

and week 3 is higher than week 2. Week 4 is generally a recovery week.
- Each 4-week block contains more intensity than the block before it. So if you have 20 weeks before the event, weeks 1-4 comprise block 1 and weeks 5-8, block 2, etc. The penultimate block will be where training intensity peaks.

If you are not training for an event, then still apply these principles. Your 'event' date might be the end of the season. If you do not operate in seasons, allocate a date in the future when you will train to. Then take some time off from SUP. This will help you to keep fresh and motivated.

A Note Of Warning To The Enthusiast! The Sins Of Training:

Although we would advocate training to improve your physical capabilities for SUP, this has to come with a health warning because too much training, or training in the wrong way, can negate any of the positive benefits. Particular issues that you need to beware of are:

Training too hard: You are keen to make progress and believe that hard work is the answer. You regularly exhaust yourself after long sessions on the sea and overtrain on the land. This results in periodic injuries or days / weeks where you wake up feeling ill. If you are training at L2, you should be able to train at this level every day.

Insufficient time for recovery: The body needs time to make adaptations.

Insufficient care around nutrition and hydration: It goes without saying that the body needs to sustain itself during stress. Water, electrolytes, calories and protein are the fundamental constituents.

Treating training as a competition instead of preparation: If each session becomes a race between you and your friends or against a Strava segment time, you lose your training focus.

Not listening to your body: Your body is messaging you all the time. It's whether you are listening! Sore throats, runny noses, cold sores, achy joints, a pervading feeling of tiredness and faster resting heart rate are all signs of overtraining. Better to feel good and fresh every day than weary. HRV (Heart rate variability) apps can help you assess your exercise readiness. Checking your resting heart rate in the morning is another.

Not recognising the ebb and flow of energy in the body: Just like the waxing and waning of the moon, our bodies are energised differently over a month. Athletes such as Bruno Hasulyo actually pay close attention to lunar cycles. The menstrual cycle plays a part in this, and intense training around this time is to be avoided. All training plans need to contain a build-up of intensity, followed by tapering to allow the body to recover fully. This is called periodisation and is typically structured around a 4-week cycle.

Not having sufficient sleep: Sleep promotes recovery and muscle growth.

Not sticking to the plan: If you have specific events throughout the year, your training plan and its activities will reflect this. Keep your training discipline.

SUMMARY

We have attempted to cover a lot of ground in a short space. This chapter is intended to help guide you towards SUP fitness, enabling progress and enjoyment. SUP fitness is based on 4 elements – endurance, power, balance and agility. Paddling develops all four of these areas, making it highly beneficial for health.

Serious-minded paddlers will want to get into more detail than we have covered here. But the principles of L2-focussed endurance training, and plyometric-based exercises for power, balance and agility will help most paddlers improve their paddling dramatically.

Training with others can help you stick to the plan

You can download blank training templates from www.fernhurstbooks.com – search for 'Improving Your Stand Up Paddleboarding' and click on 'Additional Resources'

Examples of simple training templates

Template 1: Season goals

Goal	When	Fitness attribute required	Current capability (1-10)	Priority
Compete in 11 Cities race	Sept	Endurance	5	1
Break 1 hour 15 mins for 10km	Sept	Endurance	7	2
SUP surf	Sept	Agility	3	3

Template 2: Monthly profile

	Focus	Activity	Power	Balance & agility
Month 1	Endurance & technique	3 x L2 training Technique drills		
Month 2	Endurance & technique	3 x L2 training Technique drills		
Month 3	Endurance & technique	3 x L2 training 3 x Drills	1 x plyometric 1 x resistance	3 x Bosu ball 1 x Speed ladder
Month 4	Endurance & power	2 x L2 1 x L4 Intervals	1 x plyometric 1 x resistance	3 x Bosu ball 1 x Speed ladder
Month 5	Power & readiness	1 x L2 1 x L4 intervals	1 x plyometric 1 x resistance	3 x Bosu ball 1 x Speed ladder

Template 3: Weekly plan

	Mon	Tues	Wed	Thurs	Fri	Sat
Week 1	L2 x 90 mins	30 min plyometric session	L2 x 90 mins	All body strength session 60 mins	L2 x 90 mins	Plyometric session plus agility
Week 2	1 min L4 intervals x10	30 min plyometric session	L2 x 90 mins	All body strength session 60 mins	L2 x 90 mins	Plyometric session plus agility
Week 3	L2 x 90 mins	30 min plyometric session	L2 x 90 mins	All body strength session 60 mins	L2 x 90 mins	Plyometric session plus agility
Week 4 (Recovery)	30 sec L4 intervals x10	30 min plyometric session	L2 x 45 mins	All body strength session 60 mins	L2 x 45 mins	Plyometric session plus agility

CHAPTER 6

PARTICIPATING

There are many ways you can express yourself on a SUP. In this chapter, we look at some of the more organised avenues. Paddlers can get involved in all the areas described below – nothing is exclusive or off limits to anyone. In the following sections, we look at:

- Touring
- Racing
- SUP Yoga
- Whitewater

TOURING

Why Tour?

Exploring coastlines, loch sides or rivers by SUP allows you to see things from a unique perspective and satisfies a primal feeling of adventure. Even kayakers miss out on the view that SUP offers as the height above the water dramatically increases what you can see. The ability to carry provisions and stop off along the way makes using a SUP ideal.

Planning

The things to pay attention to when touring are:

- Tell someone where you are going and how long you will be away. The free-spirited can feel constrained by doing this, but it is an essential element of personal safety.
- Be adequately equipped with a PFD (personal flotation device), proper clothing, food, sufficient water, a fully charged phone in a waterproof pouch, leash, dry bag, money, map, shoes and torch.
- Use weather apps to choose a manageable and enjoyable route for you and your group. Check the conditions to ensure the weather won't catch you out over the trip's duration. Set yourself a rough timescale and refer to this when you are out. This will give you a feeling of progress and the ability to return in the light.
- Eat and drink properly beforehand.
- When you leave your entrance / exit point, make sure you have suitable landmarks to

refer to on your return. Sometimes the land looks very different from the water, and it is surprisingly easy to get confused about where you set off from.

- If you are exploring the coastline or caves, be wary of impediments that might damage your equipment. Never risk the integrity of your board to get closer to something!
- Use GPS to ensure you are on the right track. If you don't have a GPS, a map is essential. It is easy to become disorientated.
- If in a group, never leave someone paddling on their own.

There are many weather apps that you can download to your phone. Refer to one every time you go out paddling to plan the most sensible route. As a general rule, if you are returning to the same place, always start paddling into the wind. This way, you should be returning with the wind on your back. This is a precautionary approach in case you injure yourself, the wind gets up or you run out of energy.

There may be occasions when initially paddling into the wind may not be practical. For example, if the wind is directly offshore, keep near the shore and find the most sheltered paddling route.

Use the app to see what will happen to the wind during your session. This is important in case the wind is predicted to change direction. You don't want to go out against the wind only to get to the point of return to discover the wind has done a one-eighty at the same time!

The same applies to currents (which are always in one direction) and tides (which change direction every 6 hours). As a general rule, always start paddling against the current, so the return is easier. If possible, time your trip so that the tide is with you both ways, changing direction when you begin to return.

The swell in the sea can have quite an effect on paddling in the wind. When the swell and wind are at 90 degrees to each other, the water can get very messy. An offshore wind with one or two swell waves at angles to the prevailing wind can make for harsh paddling conditions.

Touring Groups

Touring groups meet regularly in the same manner as rambling groups. You gain a sense of community and security by going out with others. You are probably more likely to be more ambitious when venturing out as a group.

There should be a tour leader who decides on the route and duration. The leader should be suitably experienced and seek to accommodate the abilities of everyone in the group.

It is not uncommon for the group to break into smaller groups once on the water. This is fine, but there needs to be a tacit agreement that no one gets left on their own! A group normally recognises this, but it is worth incorporating this into an agreed 'group code'.

There have been some tragedies where the group organiser has not recognised how sudden changing conditions could affect the 'tour'.

Any tour needs to accommodate the abilities of everyone and build in a factor of safety for unforeseen events.

There are several courses moderated by SUP and canoe organisations that can help to improve the awareness of paddlers in this regard. Someone in the group should either be highly experienced or participate in the courses.

RACING

Why Race?

The number of races available to the SUP community is increasing each year. The Circuito Mediterraneo saw the numbers participating hit record levels last year (2021). This is encouraging, but racing still has a long way to go to appeal to mainstream SUP, so why race?

Racing is a fantastic way to challenge and test your skills: Racing matures a paddler. You become vividly aware of your abilities and in greater awe of others. Race situations give you

A SUP touring group

no choice but to face challenges and conquer them.

Racing is character-forming: Races can be very humbling and formative at the same time. Conquering adversity is difficult at the time, but you can look back on situations and say to yourself, 'It was tough, but I handled it.' Racing builds resilience, self-discipline and humility.

Racing leaves you with vivid memories that bond you to others: The shared experience of a race stays with you. Years after, you will remember the day of the big waves at Cabo De Palos or the fierce wind at Torrevieja. Races can become vivid memories and milestones in your life.

Racing creates friendship: Racing is a community. The common interest and common challenge bring people together to build lasting friendships.

Racing provides focus: A race schedule provides a focus for continued development and training.

Barriers To Getting Involved In Racing

There are a number of barriers which may prevent you getting involved in racing:

Confidence: The first barrier is questioning whether you can actually take part. No one wants to look out of place. Fortunately, SUP does not have much history and the preconceptions that accompany it. Most races welcome everyone regardless of ability. In fact, races generally cater for all skills with varying distances and courses.

Geography: The big national races tend to be in well established coastal locations, which might be some distance from your base. Make a weekend of it! Take part in some casual races and time trials beforehand. These are becoming more prevalent across all countries. These events offer a great introduction to the world of competition.

Mindset: Some people think winning is the reason for competition. If they don't think they will win, they don't take part. Forget winning: participating is the reason to race – it's a test of yourself.

Being alone: If you are the only one interested from your location, don't let it stop you. Use Facebook to meet up with racers from other areas. The SUP community is very friendly, and advice flows freely. Use it to allay any fears you might have. The atmosphere at races is very inclusive: families, kids and a host of races for different abilities. Find someone who can chaperone your first time. Enter for the experience. Observe and absorb the day: from the build-up of the race to the post-race conversation.

Types Of Race

Beach races: These occur near the shore and involve navigating a course of buoys in a series of laps. These races require a high degree of skill in navigating turns and waves. They are generally a short distance making them strategic and high intensity. They are often exciting because they have the unpredictable nature of the sea as a key ingredient. Catching or missing a wave on the way back to the finish can decide who wins.

A beach race

Distance races: These tend to be 10km upwards. The start and finish might be into the onshore break. The course will probably have elements of upwind, downwind and several buoy turns. These races are primarily endurance and involve drafting and careful choice of route.

Ultra distance races are becoming very popular, as evidenced by the continued success of the 11 Cities in The Netherlands. This race is over 200km and can be completed either over 5 days or non-stop.

A downwind race

A long distance race

Downwind races: These start at one place and end at another. They tend to be 15km upwards. Drafting is not really an option, so you will find yourself paddling alone. These can be strange experiences. You focus on catching waves while watching figures ahead and to the side of you, all engaged in their own personal battles. You have to remain focused on your own progress. Watch others too closely, and you can get frustrated, making your technique incoherent.

The Molokai is possibly the most famous downwind race in SUP. Watch clips of this on YouTube to get a flavour of superb technique from the world's best.

River races: Paddling down fast-moving rivers can be quite a thrill. In narrow areas, the opportunity to overtake is limited. The ability to read the river flow, eddies, meanders and handle rapids is advantageous. The technical challenges are unique, making these high adrenaline events.

A river race

Sprint races: These take place over short distances – generally 200m. Intense, explosive and anaerobic, sprints demand power, fitness and technique.

Connor Baxter remains the man to beat (at the time of writing), but for a demonstration of technique, watch videos of Andrey Kraytor. See the way he combines offset stance, powerful broad strokes and the ability to paddle one-sided indefinitely to understand the requirements of this discipline.

Racing Strategy
The Start
You can't win a race at the start, but you can lose it. Starts are always fast. They are chaotic, and a bad start can affect your mental state for the remainder of the race.

Starts occur on land and in the water.

Beach starts involve competitors lining up and running into the water with their boards. This requires quick feet and good technique to jump on your moving board, stand up quickly

A race line-up – to begin with go to a less crowded area – it get's pretty busy

and start paddling. You need to work on how you carry both board and paddle to get comfortable and coordinated. Some carry both in the same hand; others don't. Practice makes perfect.

Other starts take place on the water. There will usually be a couple of buoys between which is an imaginary start line. You will be required to be either standing or sitting. Sometimes there will be a current or wind to contend with. You need to consider carefully where you position yourself. It is very difficult to hold a static position on a line in moving water. So, often, it is advantageous to be a good distance behind the line and time your start with the current or wind. Being agile is a big advantage at the start as it helps you to get into the paddling position quickly.

Top paddlers decide on the best starting position based on the location of the first buoy, the sea / water and wind conditions and the depth of water. For everyone else, the start is exciting and intimidating at the same time. Here are a few quick tips for the non-pros:

The start is explosive: Make sure that your body is ready for instant high intensity. Spend at least twenty minutes before the race activating your muscles. Do a thorough warm-up by running to lift your heart rate to near race level. Do some jumping and dynamic squats. Take deep breaths with five 45 second breath holds. Perform the yoga 'Sun Salutation' (see P122) routine to activate the muscles.

Find a good place in the line-up: Unless you are a front runner, the best site is usually where the least paddlers are. This is generally at the far ends of the line-up. The water is highly confused and confusing when many paddleboards and paddlers hit the water simultaneously. This makes it difficult to get a stroke or rhythm going. Also, there are always a few fall-ins. These events can interfere with progress. These factors make going from an outside starting point the safe choice. Get your board in the line-up early.

You must practise starts as they can shape your race. Paddlers have preferences as to how they hold the board and paddle. The photos below show James practising his beach starts.

Board and paddle in same hand (individual preference)

Watch the sea on entry

Jump the first break

Once deep enough, set to mount

Push board ahead for momentum

Use body to keep board moving

Get up quickly

Switch to paddle on left to keep direction

Switch on power

You must go fast at the start. You may not want to, but if you don't, you will find yourself with paddlers who are much slower than you and detached from the paddlers you are equal to. It's a lonely position, and you are likely to end up paddling the whole race in solitary confinement.

Drafting

We discussed the skill of drafting on P65, but here are some tips for a race:

Know when to find the draft: A pattern emerges after the first 500m as paddlers look to get into the nearest draft. This is a critical moment. Make sure you identify someone you are going to tuck in behind. You will need some recovery time from the exertions of the start, and the draft is the best ticket in town.

If the person in front is slower than you would like, hitch on for a few minutes before starting your assault up the field. Your aim should be to paddle hard between drafts. Try not to leave yourself paddling alone. Don't over-exert yourself if you find yourself leading a draft train. Keep to your pace. If it's too slow, then someone else will take the head. If this happens, ensure that you can tuck in behind. Drafting can save you so much energy that it changes the entire feeling of the race.

You must go fast to catch a draft: It's hard, but you have to extend yourself if there is an opportunity to acquire one ahead. This is where interval training comes into its own!

Buoy Turns

Buoys mark the route of the race. In a technical race, there may be many to navigate requiring frequent changes in direction – either to your left or right. In distance races, there may be far fewer.

The skill to undertake a buoy turn effectively can influence your final position. It is one thing to be able to execute a buoy turn on flat water with no one else around, and another to do it surrounded by paddlers in choppy water.

Indeed, conditions may have a considerable bearing on what kind of turn you choose to execute. The step-back turn (see P59) is quickest, but in choppy water, you may be better off using the crossbow turn.

Drafting

Crossbow turn

The crossbow turn involves moving back on the board (to get the nose out of the water) and crossing the top hand over the board to sweep backwards in order to get the front of the board moving in the opposite direction. This turn lacks a good photo opportunity (as it looks ungainly) but is generally more stable. It is also slower and strategy may determine which method you adopt.

Feet go back on board to lift board's nose

Both hands have gone over the board, the blade is slowly 'dug' into the water

The waist and core resist the paddle

The board turns

The paddle goes back to the 'normal' side

Make a final sweep to take board all the way around.

If you are leading others, do not get rushed into a mistake when entering a buoy turn. It is difficult to overtake the paddler ahead at a buoy without taking a circuitous route. Once past the buoy, you must switch the pace back on to avoid being overtaken.

If you are behind others who are all using a step-back turn, you might lose them if you don't do the same! There is some risk and reward to be had here. Falling in will always lose you more time than a slower turn, but risking a faster turn to stay with the draft might still be the best option!

The wind and waves can play havoc with buoy turns. One of the most frustrating things is to actually miss the buoy and have to renavigate it. This can happen in strong side winds where the wind blows you to such an extent that you turn before you get to the buoy! To mitigate this, always give yourself extra room and allow the wind to help you around the buoy. Also beware of currents and tides.

If you are in a draft and approaching the last buoy in the race, then it is generally advantageous to be at the front. So make your move before the last buoy!

It is possible to use the board in front to help nudge your board around the buoy. However, this can cause problems if your board inadvertently jumps over the board in front and takes out its rider!

A good buoy turn technique versus a bad one can save you at least 30 seconds per buoy. In a race with ten buoys, that is 300 seconds, which, at a speed of 10km/h, is the equivalent of 800m of distance!

One paddler rounds a buoy using an open side turn with wide sweeping strokes

Another padler uses a closed side turn, using paddle strokes on the opposite side to 'pull' the board around the buoy

Pacing Yourself

Race focus: Generally, it is not practical to look at your GPS during a race. If you get the 'urge', it can work in two ways. It can incentivise you to pick up the pace, or it can get you asking questions about the level of intensity you are maintaining. Be aware of the reasons and consequences of checking the GPS before doing so!

Play to your strengths: If you are not a good sprinter or not good at catching the shore break, you need to make a move for the finish early. If leading the pack, this means catching others by surprise, either by design or accident. Sometimes, an incident can signal making a move (a fall or a sudden wake). Other times it might be making a sudden change of pace. You need to get space between yourself and the others. At this point, the race becomes 100 percent psychological. If you look strong and are increasing the gap, it does not take long to 'break' the resolve of those behind.

The Finish

As with starts, sometimes the finish is on land and at other times it is on water. As you approach the finish:

- Never look behind as you approach the finish. Focus everything on yourself and what you are doing. Races are often lost by glancing behind and miscalculating the situation.
- If the finish is on land, never jump off your board too early and make a run for the finish line through the water. The board glides faster than heavy legs can trudge! Many people have lost races by jumping off too early.
- Never give up! At the end of a race, anything can happen. Your rivals can fall, they can get tangled in their leash and they can drop their paddle. Furthermore, if there are waves, these can be caught to overtake the people in front for last-minute drama.
- Always know where your leash release tag is, and if it's a finish on land, get ready to disengage it about 20m from the spot you will leave your board.
- Race with determination to the finish line always. Finish strong and feel good about what you have achieved.

Anything can happen at the finish, keep your focus on yourself!

The Racing Mindset

Racing is not just about physical capabilities, it is also about your mind:

Being competitive: Humans have different motivations for doing the same thing. In racing, it often appears that the people having the most fun are not competing to win.

Stop and reappraise your attitude if you feel frustrated, unlucky or even jealous. We SUP for fun. Even when it's bloody hard, you are doing it for fun. Enjoy the participation, the moment and the shared experience. Laugh at what happens during the race. It's a memory, an event and a learning opportunity.

When people begin racing, they have low expectations. They just enjoy the participation and place no pressure on themselves. Then they start to train, and expectation creeps in. They might have some initial success, and then, one day, they have a bad day. They feel frustrated or disappointed. This colours their overall SUP experience. They place more pressure on themselves and start feeling anxious to achieve more. It's almost as if success has been a curse. If they don't pause to reset their motives and expectations, they become disenchanted and can possibly stop racing altogether.

Racing is not about comparing yourself with other people. Enjoy it as a personal test, and always treat yourself with love and respect regardless of the result.

This is not to say 'don't be competitive'. Competition is healthy when it creates a platform for self-improvement and learning. It is unhealthy when its focus is on other people and results.

The psychology of endurance: Do you remember being a child in the back of the car asking your parents, 'are we there yet?' The focus on time and getting to the destination seemed to make the journey interminable. Similar mind games can take place during an endurance race. Focus on the finish, and the chances are you will suffer. Focus on each stroke, and the mind will not wander but adopt a trance-like state.

Ultra runners count steps, endurance paddlers can count strokes. When Michael Booth was interviewed about winning the APP World Tour in China, he said he just focused on counting ten strokes on his left and then ten on his right. That is all. The focus on the immediate stops the mind from longing to be at the destination halfway through the journey.

In sports psychology, this zoning is called having a process focus. As well as counting strokes, paddlers can purely focus on the catch or the pull. The key is to be in the present and make no excursions into the future. The human capacity to endure is not just a physical attribute.

Race Nutrition
Eating Strategy
The anticipated duration and intensity of the event should inform your nutritional requirements. If you never intend to race for longer than a couple of hours, carbs will fuel you. Adequate intake of hydration and electrolytes are both critical factors at all distances.

Adopt an eating routine that matches as closely as possible your usual one. There is no point in taking your metabolism by surprise on race day!

An average athlete will burn 1,000 calories an hour in a race, while a pro might get closer to 2,000. That's a lot of calories to find, especially as your body cannot store more than 2,000 calories of carbs at any one time. Eating massive meals the night before an event can be counter-productive in that this will take energy to digest and affect a good night's sleep. It is better to fuel up earlier in the day before a race and eat 'normally' the night before.

Your pre-race eating and training routines should build trust in your ability to perform on the big day.

Other Considerations
Electrolytes are molecules of certain minerals that have an electrical charge. Our nervous system runs on the electricity generated by manipulating these molecules. Every function (muscle movement, breathing, digestion, thinking) requires electrolytes, so you must have a sufficient store to handle heavy physical exercise. Sweating removes them from the body, so they must be constantly replaced.

Electrolyte drinks can be made by mixing Himalayan salt with lemon juice and water. Drink one pre-race and have another one to take during the race.

Hydration packs can supply the additional water needed over long distances, but for any race below 10km (in temperatures below 20°C) you should not require water during the race.

Visualisation & Self Talk
The mind and body are interconnected. Use this to your advantage in preparing for a race. Find a quiet place, and use deep breathing techniques with eyes closed to get into a state of relaxation. Then imagine yourself at the beginning of the race. Create feelings of strength and confidence and then forward wind through the race stages. Maintain resourceful feelings as you see yourself finishing strongly. These feelings will become anchored to you on race day.

Would you rather start a competition feeling powerful and confident rather than fearful and weak? The best sportsmen use these techniques and so can you.

Furthermore, always be aware of your self-talk, especially during a race. Do not say things to yourself such as 'you idiot' or 'you've blown it now'. Be your own best coach. Keep encouraging yourself and remain positive. Even when things go badly wrong, ask how you can make the best of it.

Race Training
Training Planning
If you decide to race, make sure you devise a training plan. Refer to the section concerning training plans (P103).

Training With Others
There is something energising about training with others. There are practical advantages, such as practising drafting, that can't be done alone. But there is something more than that. Being able to share time on the water, watch the technique of other paddlers and gauge your own progress are some of the advantages. If conditions are challenging, you are more likely to push yourself when in a group. So training with others helps us question our own limitations.

It is also a social activity — even when no words are exchanged. Training with others is also incentivising. If the weather is bad, you probably would not go out on your own. But the commitment to the group means you feel you have to go. Despite or because of the bad conditions, the training turns out to be one of the best you have ever had.

Other people are also excellent channels for feedback. You may not realise your progress as a paddler until someone tells you. Being recognised by others builds our self-esteem.

In a practical sense, certain routines are easier to complete when with others. Interval training can be tough. But if you are with a group, even of different abilities, doing the intervals at the same time seems easier and more enjoyable than trying to bang them out on your own! You are more likely to complete them and do them properly!

Ultimately there is something supportive about group training. If you get the chance to do it, grab it with both hands!

Training Mindset

There is a tightrope to be walked when training. Highly driven individuals might be over-zealous and burn themselves out mentally or physically. Less motivated people might start with good intentions and soon lose the will.

Like competing, be aware of your training mindset. Reflect on why you train, and find reasons to see it not as a chore but something to be enjoyed in its own right. If you look forward to each training session, your approach will differ from going into it with feelings of 'why I am doing this?'

Having A Coach

A good coach enables improved performance and will improve your paddling. Finding a coach that works for you is crucial, as coaches have different individual approaches.

In general terms, a good coach will:

- Have excellent technical knowledge of the stroke, the ways of water and human physiology
- Be accepting of the idea that there is no one right way to paddle
- Be able to provide feedback that helps the coachee visualise and understand what they need to do differently
- Be both supportive and challenging: the coach has to find the correct time to put their arms around you and the right time to say 'come on!'
- Inspire through their own actions or practices

There must be respect and trust between both parties. This bond keeps the relationship together when circumstances get strained or misunderstandings occur. A good coach is an invaluable component to progress and should be an integral part of your training.

Training with others can be really beneficial

SUP YOGA

The practice of yoga brings about the union of universal and individual consciousness. Experience this sense of oneness, and you are said to be in 'yoga'. It dates back thousands of years and, consequently, there are many approaches. Some people will not be enamoured with the idea of combining an ancient practice with being on a paddleboard. Others will embrace it.

Most people trying SUP yoga will probably have experienced land-based practice already. They will be acquainted with the positions and need for coordinated breathing. Those with no prior knowledge, will find SUP yoga a completely new challenge.

Yoga on land is fantastic for mind and body. Yoga on a SUP board, out in the middle of a mass of water, set within a natural environment provides additional layers of enjoyment and challenge.

It is advisable to know the positions to be adopted on the board before going out. Otherwise, a beginner risks the possibility of being overwhelmed by the physical requirements to adopt novel poses while positioned on an unstable base.

It is best to build the complexity of poses progressively. Get good at the easy ones before moving on to more demanding poses. As with much that we have discussed, form creates the foundation for performance. Always be able to achieve good form in what you are doing before adding complexity.

Why SUP Yoga?

There are a number of reasons why you might want to try SUP yoga:

To get a different kind of workout: SUP yoga engages other muscles to those you would use in land-based practice.

To develop mindfulness: There is an added challenge of doing yoga on a wobbly board. It will force you to be present and intentional with all your movements.

To learn something new: Even accomplished yoga practitioners will engage in a new learning path.

Tips For SUP Yoga

Doing yoga on an unstable stand up paddleboard can be a challenge initially, so here are some tips for when you start:

Find a sheltered spot: Lots of wind and big waves can make SUP yoga really difficult and distracting. Find a place that's relatively sheltered from wind and boat traffic.

Find a private area: There's something about doing yoga on a SUP that makes people stop and take notice. If you don't like being the centre of attention, put some distance between you and the busy beach.

Move slowly: If you've done yoga on land but never on a SUP, start by moving through your poses more slowly than you're used to.

Keep a wide stance: Some styles of yoga focus on a narrow body alignment. With SUP yoga, it's helpful to use a wider stance to gain a more stable base.

Keep two points of contact with the board: Try poses that maintain at least two contact points. Also, poses that keep your body aligned across the board will feel more stable than those that put you along the board (such as Warrior I or II).

Embrace the unexpected: SUP yoga is less controlled than an on-land practice. Your board can drift, a sudden wave can set you off balance and you may fall in.

Print out a routine: Pen out a set of moves, laminate it and secure it to your board so you can reference it during your practice.

Use an anchor: This stops you from worrying about floating away from the group!

Use a board designed for yoga: You need to use a board that offers stability and rigidity to perform movements properly. Of course, if you are looking for an additional challenge, try the poses on more unstable boards!

Yoga on a SUP adds new challenges

Suggested Poses

SUP yoga requires progression. Here are our recommended beginner poses. In each pose, really press your feet into the board. Focus on your breathing and tweak your positioning to find stability before fully committing to the pose.

Downward Dog

This pose helps you find the length in your spine, has the stabilising benefit of four contact points. From tabletop (where you have hands and knees in contact with the board looking like a table) push your hips up and back and slowly straighten the legs. Look at the horizon through your arms and legs!

Plank

From downward dog, lower the hips to create a straight line down your back. Feel the load being taken by the shoulders and the strain on the abs. If this is too difficult, then lower the knees to the board – if it is too easy, lift one foot off the board at a time.

Boat Pose

A fantastic pose for developing the core. Create a v shape by sitting with arms and legs pointed into the air.

The downward dog

The plank

Boat pose

Chair Pose

This builds strength in the legs. Challenge yourself to reduce the width of your feet as you adopt the chair.

Chair pose

Bridge Pose

Start on your back with knees bent and soles of your feet on the board. Keep your feet slightly wider than hip-distance apart. Lift your hips toward the sky and bind your arms beneath. When comfortable, try lifting one leg at a time.

Bridge pose

Savasana

For a serene meditative state on the water. See picture!

Savasana

... And more advanced poses:

Low Lunge

From table top, with your hips over the handle, bring your right foot forward so your hands are either side of it. Look to the horizon for balance before walking your hands onto the knee or thigh. Once you feel stable, reach both arms to the sky. Then switch sides.

Low lunge

Wide Standing Forward Fold

From low lunge, place both hands inside the front knee and walk to the rail (side of the board). Rotate onto the ball mounds of both feet, and lower the heels toward the opposite rail. Hands should be beneath shoulders, while legs should be wider than hip-distance with your toes slightly turned in.

Wide standing forward fold

The Sun Salutation

Yoga is associated with bringing about the union of mind and body. Our breathing is the gateway for this, and any yoga move should involve attention to the body form and the breath.

Breathe in through the nose and out through the mouth. Try to constrict the throat to make a slight vibratory noise as you breathe out. This stimulates the Vagus nerve and sets off a relaxation response. Breathe in as you move upwards and breathe out as you move downwards. Maintain focus on the now and the sensations in your body. Do not allow your thoughts to wander. Take each posture slowly and to the limit of a comfortable stretch.

One of the most well-known routines in yoga is the Sun Salutation. It is a sequence

Pose 1: Sunrise pose. Stand up straight with feet together while pushing both palms together. Breathe out.

Pose 2: Raised arm. Take a breath in through the nose slowly and raise your arms and hands to the sky. Feel the spine lengthen and stretch in the abdominal region.

Pose 3: Hands to feet. Slowly exhale and drop hands to the feet by hingeing at the hips. This is a gentle stretch for the lower back – not for the hamstrings.

Pose 4: Equestrian position. Begin inhaling, drop the left leg back and let the knee drop to the floor. The front knee remains at right angles to the floor as you slowly lunge forward to raise the chest and extend the spine.

Pose 5: Downward dog. Exhale, bring the right leg back to the left leg and raise the buttocks keeping hands and feet shoulder-width apart. Keep knees straight and stretch heels into the floor. Feel stretch in hamstrings.

Pose 6: Eight limb position. Hold breath briefly, drop both knees to the floor, and bring head and chest down so that feet, knees chest, hands and chin all touch the floor. This pose transitions into...

of twelve flexion and extension poses linked together as one fluid movement. The benefits of this are:

- The internal organs of the pelvis, abdomen and chest are deeply massaged
- The spine is taken through every range of motion, including flexion, extension, lateral bending, lengthening, compression and rotation

- It helps the rib cage establish a normal range of motion, making deep diaphragmatic breathing easier
- It makes muscles more flexible through a flowing series of moves

The Sun Salutation is composed of a flowing sequence of poses shown in the photo sequence.

Pose 7: Cobra position. Inhale and raise chest and head. Use back muscles to extend and keep elbows to the side. Feel the stretch in the solar plexus and abdominals as the body extends.

Pose 8: Downward dog. Exhale, raise the buttocks keeping hands and feet shoulder-width apart. Keep knees straight and stretch heels into the floor.

Pose 9: Equestrian position. Begin the inhale and swing right leg forward and left knee to the floor.

Pose 10: Hand to feet. During the exhale, bring the left leg to the right leg keeping your feet shoulder-width apart.

Pose 11: Raised arm position. As you inhale, straighten and lift the body and reach for the sky. Take the breath in slowly and feel the spine lengthen.

Pose 12 Sunset position. During exhale, lower arms and bring the hands together in front of the chest. Make sure exhalation is complete before going into the next pose.

Important points

- Let the knees be bent in poses 3 and 10
- During the first time, bring the left leg back in pose 4 and forward in pose 9; on the second run-through, bring the right leg back in 4 and forward in 9
- In pose 7, do not push into Cobra using your arms
- Use the sequence as a warm-up and cool down for 5 to 10 minutes
- Don't rush the sequence – let the breath set the rhythm

Practise the Sun Salutation on land before going out to SUP and, if you get the opportunity, try it on a SUP yoga board.

WHITEWATER SUP

Few things in SUP give the same buzz factor as hurtling down whitewater on a board. After all the stakes are high – fall off and the chances are it is going to hurt!

The boards are suitably wide, and a river's flow can look like it will be more challenging than it actually is. But as the routes get more technical, you need to have a good selection of paddle strokes on hand to change the board direction quickly and effectively.

You will also have to be very good with your feet, adopting different stances in an instant to react to a fast-changing environment. Whitewater SUPers adopt a set of 'off-parallel' stances and can spin their boards on a sixpence.

The most important aspect is the ability to read the flow of water and understand what is causing it to behave in the way it is. It can take years to develop this – making it a fascinating challenge of mind and body.

Many people who get into whitewater SUP have previous experience with river-based kayaks and canoes. Their knowledge of fast-flowing water and some pre-existing confidence to take on intimidating situations gives them a distinct advantage.

There are essential skills that anyone undertaking whitewater SUP must obtain. These include the ability to:

- Cross a flowing river
- Maintain direction when in a flow
- Change direction when in a flow
- Run with the river when required to do so

See the offset stance of the whitewater paddler

These skills are best acquired under expert tuition. They require the employment of advanced paddle strokes and the acquisition of confidence built through incremental progress. Paddling in whitewater is not something to do solo. Always be adequately protected and wear headgear. Be prepared to get wet as you learn the unique way in which a SUP board interacts with flowing water.

Types Of Whitewater SUP

There are various modalities of whitewater SUP:

Down-river: Entering a river at a certain point (called a put-in) and travelling downstream to another spot (the take-out). A down-river trip can consist of rapids, drops, surf waves or even waterfalls. Elements of adventure and problem solving are always around you. The whitewater environment is dynamic: varying water levels, for example, can alter the difficulty, turning a gentle stream into a raging torrent.

Surfing standing waves: Under certain circumstances, the flow of water constricting and flowing over rocks causes the formation of standing waves. The water recirculates and propels you forward on these features as the rest of the river flows beneath you. Standing waves offer inland paddlers a place to experience the thrill of catching and riding waves similar to those in the ocean. While a typical ocean wave might only last a few seconds, standing waves give you the chance to surf for extended periods.

The larger the wave, the faster you will be moving across its face, making it more difficult to stay in control. Higher speeds and more prominent wave faces offer the chance for more dynamic turns and surfing. Regardless of the wave's size, you must be very careful to understand what lies beneath the wave and downstream before attempting to surf. The dangers of whitewater environments are often subtle or even invisible.

Down-river white water SUP

Surfing a standing wave

Competitive races (such as SUP X): These races involve navigating complex flowing water, eddies, counter-currents and gates against the clock. The race scene is big in the USA and is growing in Europe. The UK hosts a few major events a year, and its popularity is growing. It's fast, fun and physically draining.

A SUP X race

Finding Suitable Places

Although it may seem like a highly specialised and inaccessible sport, the opportunities for whitewater paddleboarding are more significant than most people realise. Whitewater rafting and kayaking are established practices and a network of information is already in place.

Guide books and online references can be helpful in finding the best destinations in your area. They will also provide the optimum flow levels, grade of difficulty and helpful information about hazards, access and even driving directions. Consult websites and apps for the locations. There is a network of whitewater enthusiasts across the UK that can be found in Whitewater SUP Facebook groups.

Having A Paddling Partner

Most whitewater activities are best done with at least one other person. This is practical from a logistical point of view for transportation reasons and safety. It is also much more fun having a companion to share the rush of conquering new challenges.

If you are a novice, paddle with an expert or highly experienced partner. The stakes are much higher in this activity than a leisurely paddle on a lake!

Having The Right Gear

We look into equipment in Chapter 7. Whitewater SUP is more demanding on equipment than any other form of SUP. Choose a board that allows you to achieve your paddling goals and express your style on the water. There are some well established brands in this area such as NRS, Fanatic, Balfish and Hala. The Hala Pena is an incredible piece of inflatable engineering.

Inflatable boards offer a rigid, lightweight and versatile platform with unsurpassed durability. Slamming into rocks and being pinned against boulders are circumstances inflatable boards can withstand. The option of deflating and stowing the board in small spaces is another advantage. These benefits make inflatable SUPs an excellent choice for paddlers looking to handle almost any whitewater scenario.

The only time not to pick an inflatable is if you intend to do freestyle tricks in a deep, high-volume surf wave. Then a solid epoxy board comes into its own.

Start with a board with plenty of volume and stability. As your skills progress, you can try smaller shapes, forgoing stability for manoeuvrability and performance.

When choosing a paddle for whitewater, you must find a blade with high durability. You will almost certainly be stabbing unseen rocks, river bottoms and other damaging situations. Carbon fibre isn't necessarily the most durable or appropriate option in whitewater. Instead, fibreglass blends with reinforced blades are a better choice. It is also worth considering using a two-piece paddle with an adjustable shaft – to vary the shaft length according to the conditions ahead of you: longer for a river run and shorter in rapids.

There are choices to be made in clothing from wetsuits and drysuits. A 6mm wetsuit offers the best all-around solution (cost, practicality), but a drysuit (while it can be more easily damaged) offers the warmest option!

You will need neoprene boots, gloves and a cap. If you are going to operate at a more extreme level, then a full-face helmet, shin and elbow guards are all required to protect you from the inevitable falls.

The choice of leash is critical in whitewater SUP. Not only are you more likely to fall off, you are also more exposed to potential life-threatening hazards than other forms of SUP.

The board can become wedged in an obstruction (such as a rock). In such a situation, you must be able to detach yourself from the board quickly and easily – making the need to wear a quick-release waist belt imperative. You must ensure the waist leash is fitted correctly and any excess belt material cut off (to avoid snagging issues). You must know how to use the belt before you go out – so practise releasing yourself in a safe area before entering a challenging environment. In situations where low-hanging branches are likely to get tangled up with the leash coil, it might be safer not to wear one at all.

Wearing the right gear for the job

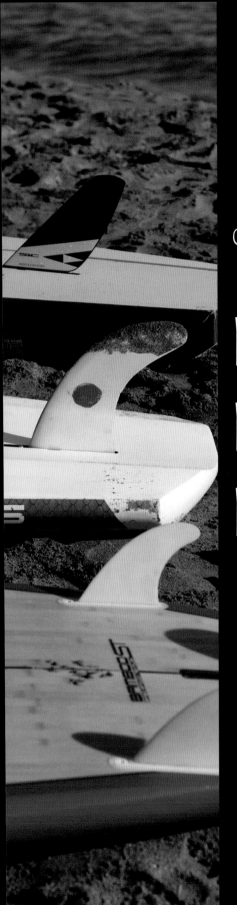

CHAPTER 7

BEING PROPERLY EQUIPPED

Serious SUPing can entail considerable financial investment. As well as the board, paddle and leash, many other equipment requirements must be accommodated. Like most things, you generally get what you pay for. Your purchase decisions can be life-saving; therefore, always seek to get the best you can for your budget. The board will probably be the highest cost, but a high-quality paddle, drysuit or wetsuit are not cheap.

What you decide to invest in depends on your budget and what type of SUP you plan to do. Do not skimp on the essentials:

■ A good quality board
■ A paddle and leash
■ A PFD (personal flotation device)
■ High-performance clothing

BOARDS

Never buy a board without trying it first. If you cannot afford a high-quality new board, buy a second-hand one.

Go for a leading brand as these companies have invested heavily in building solid reputations; they cannot risk years of brand equity by putting their names on poor-quality boards. A second-hand branded board is a better buy than a new non-branded one. The leading brands in Europe (in no particular order) are Fanatic, SIC, Starboard, One, 404, 425 Pro, NSP, RRD, Redwood Paddle, Naish, Mistral and Red Paddle.

There are also less well-established brands that sell good quality gear. Read reviews and ask questions about them on Facebook groups. Be wary that there are also brands that cater to low-cost, high-volume markets whose products are only usable as leisure craft.

Most boards are manufactured in the Far East. The premium brands invest in design and innovation and utilise more exotic materials to enhance performance.

Elite sport drives innovation. This is good news for the consumer because they get to use more and more sophisticated equipment as a consequence.

If you are relatively new to the sport, buying a second-hand board allows you to spend more on essential life-saving kit (and getting a good paddle). It provides the opportunity to upgrade in the future without significant sunk costs. For example, race boards that cost £2,500 can be bought for £1,000 on the second-hand market.

Buying your first board is always a challenge. You can get overwhelmed by the huge choice, abundant advice from others and seductive internet reviews. Take your time, try different boards and buy something that you can sell again easily. If you are keen and develop your skills quickly, it might only be 6 months before you are looking for something better.

Owning more than one board can be seen as a bit of a luxury, but it is justifiable to have a choice of boards to match different conditions or just to play around with. Your board becomes your best friend. You will go through many experiences together. Sometimes they are hard to give up!

The popularity of SUP has caused an exponential growth in board manufacturers and a comprehensive range of board types. The inflatable market dominates sales growth. Major retailers estimate that over 90 percent of their sales come from this market.

Solid Or Inflatable

Sales of inflatables dominate the SUP market because they have broad appeal as they are easy to transport and use. Inflatables can be folded into a rucksack, making them easily transportable and not needing much space for storage. They also make the ideal board to start learning to SUP because they are 'soft' (if you fall onto them) and easy to get back onto if you fall off. The materials that are used to make them are improving all the time and they can withstand a fair amount of mistreatment. It is claimed by inflatable sales teams that inflatables now perform as well as solid boards, but this is not really the case.

Most people use inflatables for leisure and touring. Rigidity is a prerequisite of performance, and inflatables, even when constructed of advanced drop-stitch materials and inflated to high pressure, are inherently 'bouncy'. Even the premium boards made stiffer with plastic inserts are more 'bouncy' than their solid counterparts.

Inflatables are becoming more advanced in shape and materials, but their shaping will always be more limited than solid construction. Subtle curves, changes in hull shape, varying the height of rails and changing the volume in the nose are all difficult to accommodate. Most inflatable designs of a given length are very similar.

Although the materials used are hard-wearing, inflatables are burstable when in use. They can fail when you least want them to. Valves can leak and joints unravel. If you leave them out in the sun, the changes in air pressure can deform the board irreparably.

Unless they are a premium brand, inflatables lose value quickly. They do not have the expected life of a solid board.

Solid boards are made of wood, plastic, glass fibre and / or derivatives of carbon fibre. They can be designed and shaped for a specific purpose. The materials used are both light and strong. However, solid boards can be damaged. While carbon fibre is strong, at the same time, it is easy to dent or fracture with paddles or overtightening the roof rack straps!

Solid boards are less affected by the wind and more responsive to turn. They are faster, have a better glide, are better to surf and are more reliable for long trips. In our opinion, solid boards have more character and give the rider more of a thrill each time you get on them.

OK, you can see where we stand on this but, as we have said, what is important is to find the construction that is right for you and what you intend to do with your board, which is what we will cover next.

Categorisation

SUP boards can be defined by the following use categories:

General-Use Leisure

Usually 10ft to 12ft in length and 30 plus inches in width.

These make great first time boards, are easy to use and learn on and can do most things on the water in a limited fashion.

Inflatables make fantastic first-time boards

Touring

Length 12ft to 14ft, width 26 to 30 inches.

These boards are very stable and have decent glide. Designed to be easy to use for longer trips on the water, with tie-down areas to secure bags.

Touring boards are both long and relatively wide, providing good glide and storage capability

Race

Length 12ft 6in to 14ft, width 20 to 26 inches.

Made out of lightweight materials, these boards are designed for speed. There is a range of designs specific to flatwater or rough sea conditions. These boards can be used for touring at more generous widths.

Race boards are longer and thinner, in width, than other boards and made of the lightest, strongest materials

Downwind

Length 14ft to unlimited, width 23 to 28 inches.

These boards are designed to catch waves with the wind behind them. Narrow tails, big noses and varying degrees of rocker enable these boards to go faster than probably any other paddleboards on the market. Some boards even have foot steering mechanisms.

Downwind boards are designed to catch ocean waves

Yoga

Length 10ft, width 34 inches.

These are specialist boards with a shape reflecting the need for stability. They are not rectangular but are close – with a wide nose and wide tail and 6 inch parallel rails (to keep you dry). These boards have an exceptionally high volume for length.

Yoga boards need to be stable and provide a dry platform

SUP Surf

Length 7ft to 10ft, width 29 to 34 inches.

These are specialist boards to be used only in waves. There is a range of shapes, sizes and widths. If you are new to SUP surf, get something with plenty of width to help with stability. These boards have multiple fin arrangements and low rails to carve turns. (See also P137 – SUP Surf Or Longboard.)

SUP surf boards are short and agile

Whitewater

Length 9ft to 11ft, width 30 to 34 inches.

These are specialist boards designed to handle the rigours of white water. Inflatables work best in this environment.

Whitewater boards need to be manoeuvrable and durable

Multi-person

Length 15 feet upwards, width 34 inches upwards.

These boards are generally inflatable and are used for leisure and racing. They generally accommodate from 2 to 8 people. The Red 'Dragon class' is 22 feet and has nearly 1,000 litres of volume. If you are interested in a group activity or team bonding, these boards definitely bring people together.

Multi-person boards offer a different kind of involvement in SUP

Key Factors That Affect Board Performance

Length

SUP boards range from less than 7 feet for surf SUP to unlimited (but usually 17 feet for single-person use). Popular lengths are 10 feet for general use and 14 feet for racing and touring. The longer the board, the more extensive the glide, but the less manoeuvrable a board is.

14 feet boards have excellent tracking ability and are well proportioned for people weighing 70kg upwards. For smaller / lighter people, 12ft 6in boards might be better suited to their size and weight.

Short SUP surf boards are fantastically responsive but have minimal volume. Consequently, you need to have good balance and keep the board moving to avoid submerging.

Width

Width affects stability. Race boards designed for the flat (or used by pros) might be 20 inches wide. Narrower boards tend to be less stable. A good starting width for general use is probably 24 inches. This goes up to 34 inches for specific SUP and general-use boards.

SUP surf boards can be wide compared to their length, making them stable (when accompanied by volume) and manoeuvrable. But these proportions make them arduous to paddle any distance as they are designed to catch waves in the drop.

Volume

Volume provides an idea of how much load a board can support. A 26 inch wide and 14 foot long board might have 320 litres of volume; a 7-foot stubby SUP surf less than 100 litres. A 100kg rider would comfortably stand on the former but sink without a trace on the latter!

Board designers distribute the volume of a board to the nose and tail in different ways. A downwind board is generally designed to pop out of the waves and will have more volume in the nose than a flat water board where this action is not required.

Every board needs some volume in the tail to counterbalance the nose, otherwise they may feel unbalanced and tricky to trim.

Weight

Boards seem to vary in weight from 8kg to 14kg. Anything over 12kg starts to feel heavy to carry for any distance. Some boards feel heavy to carry because their handle is poorly located or designed.

Make sure the weight of the board is acceptable to you. Also, a heavy board can be a sign of water ingress, so always be mindful of the board's weight.

Rocker

If you place a SUP board on a flat surface, you will see some curvature at the nose and tail. The degree of curvature is known as the rocker.

The flatter the board, the more the rider's weight is distributed across the whole surface area. These boards are well adapted to be used on flat water, where they will sit higher in the water and have less drag, making them faster. However, when catching waves or downwinding, a more pronounced rocker tends

to come into its own. The shape makes it easier to keep the nose out of the water and trap waves.

All-round boards are basically a compromise between flat water and downwind.

Most surf SUP and general-use boards have a degree of rocker to make it easy to handle variable water conditions.

Hull Design

You will probably have heard of the terms 'planing' and 'displacement' hulls. These terms are really used to describe the hulls of boats. In simple terms, a trawler might have a displacement hull and a speedboat a planing hull. Displacement hulls sit in the water and displace the water by virtue of different cross-section shapes, ranging from v shapes to semi-circular. Planing hulls rely on a boat reaching a certain speed to rise out of the water and bounce on top of it (known as planing).

Hulls on SUPs are generally all predominantly flat bottomed. However, to get a board on the plane requires a speed of 13km/h – a speed you will only achieve catching significant bumps on a downwinder. So why do we have planing hulls on boards that don't actually plane? It's a question of practicality –

Note the difference in the rocker (curvature) between these three boards

as forming a V-hull on a SUP would make it a challenge for anyone to stand on!

Designers are constantly seeking ways to improve performance. They introduce subtle shapes in the hull to change the way the water flows under the board. Some hulls have a concave or a double concave. Some hull edges are more rounded than others. These modifications definitely affect how a board feels.

Starboard and NSP seem to be particularly innovative in this area – creating double concaves and rounded edges. SIC and Fanatic appear to be more conservative in their approach with flatter, simple hull shapes.

All boards perform well in most conditions and have unique advantages in particular situations. Do not get too hung up on the debate concerning displacement and planing hulls. Try out a few boards and go with the one that feels right for you.

Starboard Freestyle with a 'catamaran' style hull

SIC RS with a virtually flat hull

Nose

Some boards have a sharp nose designed to displace the water as they move forward. These are often used in flat water boards.

Some boards have a more rounded nose that sticks out of the water. Lifting the nose out of the water creates a different bow wave shape. These boards seem faster to accelerate but are slower at all-out speed.

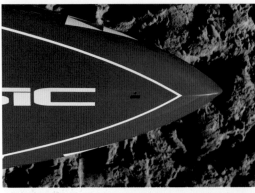

The sharp nose is designed to punch through the water

The raised rounded nose is designed to get above the water and provide lift

Rails

The rails are basically the sidewalls of the board. Rails on 14-foot boards tend to be quite pronounced and high compared to those on surf SUPs which can be just the thickness of the board and rounded in profile. Sharp rails dig in and keep a board tracking in a straight line. Rounded rails are easier to direct. Sharp rails give less of a feeling of 'tippiness'.

High rails allow a board to contain a large volume in a narrow width. The popular Starboard Allstar is an excellent example of this. High rails are affected by the wind and can act as small sails in big gusts.

Rails on inflatables tend to be 4 or 6 inches. 6 inches will keep your feet drier but might catch more wind.

High rails on a race board

Low rounded rails on a SUP surf board

Tails

You will notice a wide range of tails, from pin tails, square tails and fifty-pence-piece tails. Each tail creates turbulence which slows the board down. Designers are constantly studying ways to minimise this. There are so many different shapes – which tells you that there is no universal solution.

Pin tail on F-One downwind board

Square tail on Starboard Allstar

Fifty-pence-piece on a SIC Atlantis

Pin tails are generally found on downwind boards. These tails have less volume at the back and therefore allow the nose to keep out of the water by being less prone to pitch into waves. Square tails are often found on flat water boards, where the benefits of maximum length outweigh using any other tail shape. It is said that square tails are more stable for a step back turn, but pin tails offer less resistance at the tail – so do seem to spin round more quickly.

All-purpose boards seem to go for a compromise between the two, with fifty-pence-piece shapes (as seen in the SIC Atlantis).

Surf SUP boards have an array of tails, including fish tails. If you are just starting SUP surf, opt for a tail shape you are familiar with. As you build up skill and feel, experiment with more advanced tail shapes.

Other Factors To Consider
Flat Deck Or Dugout

A flat deck has a relatively uniform thickness. The deck feels flat from front to back. You can hang your toes off the edges if you like. A flat deck feels 'natural' to most people. They are easy to walk up and down on.

A dugout has a deck where your feet are 'sunk' into the board. Your feet are closer to the water, making you more stable. The dugout depth usually reduces to the tail, so you find yourself stepping on an inclining surface as you go back. This makes lifting the nose of the board out of the water easier.

You will find your feet can steer a board more easily in a dugout, but at the same time, it might feel more tippy. You might get a better catch as your feet are virtually level with the water.

Dugouts are much more challenging to get back into if you fall in. You might also find that they are easy to damage as they have high rails and thin top edges that form the dugout. These edges are easily damaged by errant strokes and clumsy attempts to get back in!

Flat deck on Starboard Freestyle

Big dug out on F-One downwind

If you are progressing from an inflatable to a solid board, it might be best to go to a flat deck in the first instance.

Volume At The Front

A large volume at the front of the board keeps the board's nose from burying when you are in the waves. It helps you catch waves and feels stable in the chop. However, going into the wind is more challenging as the prominent nose offers resistance to the wind and can easily be dislodged off the intended route.

Hollow Or Solid

Hollow boards owe their heritage to performance kayaks. They have an advantage over solid boards because they are lighter with a similar stiffness. However, they cannot be shaped to the same degree as a solid board.

If you are looking for all-out speed, especially in the flat, a hollow board might be the way to go. But they are easily damaged and not easy to repair, making them impractical for most paddlers.

Carbon Or Composite

Carbon is light and strong but fragile to impact damage. Composite materials are almost as lightweight, nearly as strong and more forgiving if damaged. Carbon is worth the extra money if you are racing, and composite is perfect if you are not.

Surf SUP Or Longboard

Surf SUP boards have evolved from surfboards and share many of their characteristics. They are short, wide and sexy. They are higher volume than a surfboard and come in many configurations.

SUP longboards are longer, narrower and more classical. They are similar in appearance to the surfboards of the 60s. They are faster in the water than their stubby compatriots, a reason some paddlers might find them easier to catch waves on.

Both these types of boards offer great fun in the waves. They turn and manoeuvre like no other type of SUP board.

Unusual shape of Starboard Hypernut

Traditional shaping of Starboard Pinetek

Sea, Loch Or River?

If you are paddling predominantly in the sea, go for a solid board if at all possible. The sea is a variable and temperamental environment. Once the wind is up, or the chop is out, a solid board is the only board you want to be on.

If you are predominantly paddling on a lake or loch, where the conditions are more benign, then inflatables can work well.

When paddling rivers, inflatables can come into their own. Rivers offer a varied environment with patches of calm water, running water and rapids. If you have a small fin set up, you can paddle in very shallow environments. Inflatables can take more impact damage than a solid one in this environment, and paddling a 12ft 6in, 29-inches wide touring inflatable is perfectly achievable down most rivers. This gives a good balance between glide, durability and agility.

Whitewater paddling with big drops and complex runs requires a specialist white water board.

Board Attachments

The choices don't stop with the board, then there are then all the attachments to it.

Fins

Fins are a science in themselves. The fin opposes the turning forces the paddler creates with each stroke. Fins, along with rails, keep you straight. The larger the surface area of a fin, the more force it can redirect and, therefore, the better the tracking. But the price to be paid for a larger surface area is more drag – which will slow you down.

The deeper and thinner (in profile) a fin, the easier the board will turn. This makes this shape good in beach races. The shallower the fin and smaller the surface area, the more unstable but faster the board will be. Flexible, shallow fins are necessary on river trips where shallow water will be encountered.

Fins come in a variety of shapes. The shapes reflect experimentation and practicality. Fins with a sleek angle are often termed 'weedless' fins as they are designed to prevent being clogged up by organic material.

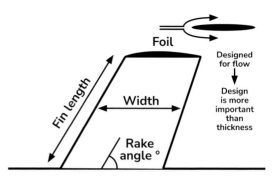

	Area	Depth	Length	Rake angle
High ↑	Stability	Turning	Stability & Tracking	Turning
Low	Speed	Speed	Speed	Anti-drift

Materials

Carbon Fibre	**Race & High Performance**
Glass Fibre	**River & General**
Plastic	**General**

Fin design

Fins come in many shapes, sizes and set-up

The material of a fin is critical to its performance. A bendy plastic fin will not resist the forces and leverage you put on it to the same degree as one made of carbon fibre. Most high quality fins are composite / carbon fibre to make them strong and durable. Fins do get damaged regularly, both while paddling and in transit.

When you become more advanced, the finer details of fin performance will become more relevant. Fins are expensive, and you don't need an array of them. One high quality general-purpose one will suffice for most paddlers.

SUP surf boards and some leisure boards have multiple fins arrangements. This provides flexibility in the way you set the board up. As a general rule, multiple fins provide a greater turning ability. Something ideal for spinning the board around quickly to catch waves.

Intuitively you would assume that more fins slow a board down, but experiments by Bryce Dyer in *SUPboarder* magazine seemed to debunk that. However, race boards have not adopted multiple fin arrangements to increase speed, so the general verdict is one fin for speed and multiple fins for manoeuvring.

Most boards have a US fin box to accommodate the replacement of the fin that came with the board.

Innovative fins are finding themselves on the market – such as those produced by a Spanish company called Keillor. These are hollow and incorporate a pressure differential mechanism claimed to increase board speed.

Deck Pads

You stand on the deck all the time when SUPing, so it's nice to stand on something comfortable and grippy. Some deck pads really work well, and others seem like an afterthought.

Make sure you are happy with the deck pad on any board you contemplate purchasing. It needs to feel right for you. Deck pads can be replaced with aftermarket products, but care must be taken removing the old one and fitting the new one.

Replacement deck material

Handles

Some handles just work better than others. This is a personal preference item, but you might spend a fair amount of time carrying your board – so make sure you find the handle arrangement acceptable to you.

The SIC Atlantis handle – the best handle ever?

More common fabric handle

Pressure Relief Valves

These valves are located on solid boards and are designed to relieve excess pressure inside the board that can build up through rising changes in temperature. Solid boards generally have some kind of polystyrene-like filling – so there is lots of air.

Air expands rapidly with changes in temperature, which, left unattended, can deform a board. Some valves are manual and others automatic. Have a SUP routine that includes loosening the valve after use and tightening it before going on the water again. If you have an automatic valve, these can go wrong, so check your board now and again to ensure that no deformities appear.

Pressure relief valves on a solid board – automatic (top) and manual (bottom)

How To Pick A SUP Board

Many variables influence performance, making buying your first (or tenth) board a matter of research, experimentation and compromise.

You need to be very clear about what you are buying a board for. For example, you might buy a fast, narrow board only to find that you cannot use it in your local area because the sea conditions are always too rough for you. Alternatively, you buy a friend's short wide board and soon realise that you cannot keep up with the touring group you go out with at the weekend.

As the last few pages have shown, there are an almost overwhelming amount of variables to consider when choosing a board, alongside budget considerations. To try to cut through this, here are some basic questions you need to ask yourself when choosing a board:

Q.1. What will you use it for?

As we have seen, board shapes range from very specific to general:

- A SUP surf board of 9 feet is the king of the waves, but try going out with a touring group and you will be talking to yourself
- Buy a general board and think that you will be surfing with the cool dudes and you will be disappointed
- A 20-inch race board might look magnificent and be on the market at an unbelievable price, but unless you are highly talented or an up-and-coming pro, you will never stand on it; you will also find it difficult to sell

So you need to be clear about what your main interest is and not get intoxicated by a deal, a brand or an impractical ambition.

Q.2. Where can you store it and how will you transport it?

Obvious questions that will influence whether you buy inflatable or solid. While we may argue that usually 'solid is best', that's no good if you haven't got anywhere to put it!

Q.3. What length, width and volume will best suit you?

This will reflect your physical size, current SUP abilities and what you are intending to do on it. The previous pages should help you answer this question.

Q.4. Can you grow into it?

Be realistic. Don't buy a board that you can't stand up on, but don't buy a board you can do a handstand on either! Buy a board that will challenge and teach you.

PADDLES

There is an abundance of paddles to choose from. The paddle is an item that you have to love. Never skimp or compromise on your choice. The adopted height for a paddle is generally between 2 and 8 inches above the top of the head, when you are standing beside the paddle. For SUP surf, this reduces to head height.

There are several factors to consider when selecting a paddle:

Weight

Use a light paddle and you will find it very difficult to ever go back to a heavier one. The weight of a paddle can take its toll over the kilometres. Light paddles will save you energy and stem the onset of fatigue. They facilitate higher cadence and are easier to undertake a full range of strokes.

The most lightweight paddles weigh 450g, while an aluminium three-piece weighs approximately 1kg. Never has half a kilogram difference felt so heavy!

Material & Construction

The best paddles are all made from carbon fibre or carbon fibre composites. The composite helps provide some flex in the shaft and reduces the chance of injury.

The best performing paddles are all single piece as there is no compromise in their structural integrity. However, sometimes it is necessary to opt for two or three-piece paddles:

- Opt for a two-piece if you have not decided on your ideal paddle length
- Opt for a three-piece if you do a lot of travelling, requiring a small carrying size

Yes, there are aluminium paddles that can be used, but the difference is so vast that we could not recommend anyone really interested in SUP to spend much time paddling with them. They are heavy and will affect both your technique and chances of injury.

Handle

The handle is in contact with your hands virtually the entirety of every outing. It needs to feel comfortable and be practical in terms of fit and ease to twist. Selection is therefore very much a personal choice. Handles vary in width and profile. Some are designed specifically for SUP surf and have an asymmetrical shape to ensure you know immediately whether the blade is facing in the right direction.

Prolonged paddling can damage the fleshy pad in the palm of your hand, so making sure the handle fits well with your hand is really important to avoid a nagging injury.

You'll be holding the paddle handle all the time, so make sure it's comfortable – here are two different styles

Shaft

The shaft needs to be stiff to conduct power and have a degree of flex. Without sufficient flex, your shoulders are likely to get injured.

You roll the shaft in your fingers with every stroke, therefore the shaft needs to feel comfortable in your hands.

Shafts vary in diameter and profile shape (circular or ovoid). Some are even tapered. These variations are catering for personal preferences.

There are also shafts which have an offset in them which are designed to improve the catch phase. While these appear to make a lot of sense in theory, they don't seem to have been attractive to most of the world's best paddlers. But they might work for you!

The Blade

The blade is often the most talked-about component of a paddle. Two main shapes have been adopted by manufacturers: rectangular and teardrop. The idea of both these shapes is to enable smooth entry and exit of the blade into the water.

The blade will be offset by 10 degrees (plus or minus). This is to create a positive angle between the blade and water to create 'up lift' at insertion.

Paddle faces tend to have a scoop, a dihedral or both! Any blade will probably work for you, but you will need to adjust your stroke or timing to get the best out of them. They will all behave slightly differently in the water:

■ The scoop is designed to catch more water

Paddle blades vary in shape, cross-sectional area and geometry

and you may feel quite a sudden lock in the water

- The dihedral offers a less sudden lock and smoother transmission of power

Blade areas vary from 70 to 90 square inches. The bigger the blade size, the more physical power you will need to paddle with it. Large area blades are often used for surfing, sprinting and shorter distances. Smaller area blades are used for longer distances.

A small area paddle with a scoop can still give you plenty of power, and many high quality paddlers will use blades as small as 77 square inches for endurance races. Many experienced SUP surfers now opt for smaller blade areas with shorter shaft length paddles. They revert to high cadence to build speed quickly to match the speed of the waves.

Many paddlers make the mistake of opting for greater blade area in the belief that it will result in more power. If their technique is not good enough, they will just toil and run the risk of injury.

CLOTHING

What you wear will reflect the conditions, expected weather and the likelihood you will be in the water rather than on it. The correct clothing is essential for your enjoyment and safety. There have been tragedies where paddlers have embarked on expeditions inappropriately dressed. They have encountered difficult conditions, ended up in the sea, and died of exposure in a surprisingly short period.

Paddling while feeling either cold or hot is not desirable. But at least when you are hot, you can de-layer. When you are cold and wet, and the wind is blowing through you, it can affect how you experience SUP. Always dress for the worst expected weather and be prepared to lose a layer.

Modern clothing is phenomenal in its

performance qualities. Good quality gear can now protect you in all weather eventualities and is well worth the extra investment.

Long sleeve top (above); trousers (below)

Two piece kit like this offers protection from the wind and a good range of motion

Quick-dry technical shirts are great on warm summer days

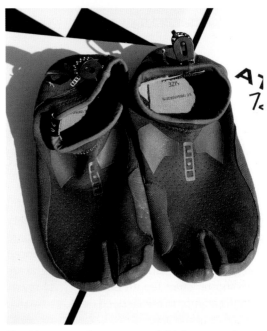

Booties come in a range of thicknesses for different uses; you lose some feel with the board when you wear them, but on some days they just have to be worn!

Wetsuits come in a range of thickness and shapes

There are many drysuits on the market making choosing one a difficult task

Basic guidance for clothing in cold conditions with water temp 4 to 8°C:

	Body	Feet	Hands	Head
Touring	2mm long-john wetsuit with windbreaker top	6mm neoprene boots	Neoprene gloves	Waterproof beanie
Race	Long sleeve neoprene blended top with neoprene windbreaker Neoprene / blend trousers	Neoprene boots or shoes or 'woven socks'	Woven merino lined gloves	Waterproof beanie
River	Drysuit with a thermal underlayer (can get damaged) 4mm wetsuit Possibly knee & elbow pads	7mm neoprene boots with hard bottom	Neoprene gloves	Neoprene hood & helmet
Surf SUP	5mm neoprene wetsuit	6mm neoprene boots	Neoprene mitts	Neoprene hood

Conditions warm and sunny, water above 12°C:

	Body	Feet	Hands	Head
Touring	Quick-dry shorts Base layer & overtop	Neoprene shoes to allow you to beach	Bare	
Race	Quick-dry top & shorts	Bare feet	Bare	
River	Drysuit or quick-dry two piece	Neoprene boots	Gloves	Beanie & helmet
Surf SUP	2mm armless wetsuit with light technical overtop	Bare feet	Bare	

OTHER ESSENTIAL PIECES
OF EQUIPMENT

Leash

Leashes are attached at either the ankle, calf or waist. All locations work reasonably well and personal preference will dictate. Ankle and calf leashes should never be worn on rivers or anywhere where the board might get stuck in an obstacle. There have been some tragic situations of paddlers drowning because they could not get to the leash to release them from their board while stuck in fast-flowing water. In such circumstances, a quick-release waist leash is the only option.

Ankle leash coiled

Ankle leash straight

Waist leash coiled

Waist leashes are preferred by some paddlers because:

- They are easier to reach and to take off quickly
- They don't trail along the back of the board (getting in the way of your feet for step back turns)
- The board does not go as far from you when you fall off

Ankle leashes are worn straight (as opposed to coiled) in surf situations. This helps keep the board as far away from you as possible if you fall off. SUP surf leashes need to be strong, so opt for an 8mm thick urethane material. Leash length matches the size of the board typically.

Leashes are generally attached to the tail of the board. However, they can be connected in front of the feet. If you are not falling in, this is a very practical place to attach them.

There may be times when you encounter high winds. You want to know that the board will still be near you if you fall in. Cheap leashes will break under the stresses of such conditions and could leave you in a very vulnerable situation.

In whitewater situations, there may be a choice as to whether to wear a leash or not. We suggest:

- Wear one in low risk of entanglement situations – such as surfing river waves or running deep high flow rivers (where you really don't want to lose your board!)
- Decide not to wear one at all in high risk of entanglement areas – where steep drops, technical rapids, rocks, trees and other obstructions pose a real danger even when wearing a quick-release mechanism

Personal Floatational Device

This piece of kit could literally save your life. In the circumstances, buy one that is visible, easy to paddle in and well made. This might mean you spend three times more than the cheapest option, but it will be money well spent. If you buy a heavy and uncomfortable basic lifejacket, you will be less likely to wear it. Some of the jackets on the market are made to protect you but be almost unnoticeable.

There are waist-located PFDs that inflate by a single-use gas cylinder. These seem like a paddler's dream as they are far less awkward to wear than a vest. However, these devices require attention and time to put on and inflate in an emergency. You might not have the time or ability to do this in certain difficult situations. The inflated vest is very flimsy. A personal view, but these devices do not offer the same level of protection as a standard vest.

A personal flotation device, which could save your life

Waterproof Pouches

These are really handy for keys, phones, money and valuables.

Waterproof pouch

Hydration Pack

These can be located on your back, in a PFD or across the waist. There are many on the market, and most are not designed with paddling in mind. Find a design where the teat can be easily accessed when paddling, otherwise, your rhythm will be constantly lost during drinking.

The bladder material can quickly become contaminated with mould, so if you are not planning on using yours for a while, store it in the freezer – after thoroughly cleaning it, of course.

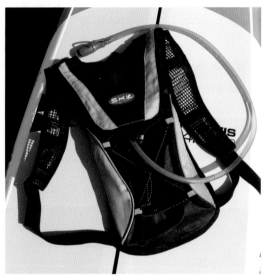

Hydration pack

Apps

A host of apps can also be used in conjunction with GPS watches. Strava is an excellent app to follow fellow athletes and even create a community of paddlers. This app is strangely inspirational, as you receive kudos from others and can observe how much activity they are engaged in.

Some apps can help you plan your route, providing information on winds, tides, waves and even river depth. Others can help you in an emergency by assisting the relevant services to locate you quickly.

GPS Watch

There are many GPS devices on the market. They are an essential piece of kit as they can provide you with vital information, including:

- Heart rates in zones for training
- Stroke rates
- Top and average speed
- Route and distance travelled

You can interrogate your performance and build up a picture of possible improvement areas. If you use the 'share' apps on these devices, you can also see how your fellow paddlers perform.

GPS watches are great for helping with training. The heart rate graphs after an interval session provide fantastic feedback on performance.

GPS watches are also helpful in tracking where you are and how to get back.

Wax

The paddle shaft can become slippery in certain conditions because of sweat or water. Many paddlers use wax to provide a non-slip surface in such circumstances. Depending on the ambient temperature you are paddling in, there are various wax preparations to choose from. Some are made for cold weather and others for warmer climates. Wax helps you keep a consistent rhythm as it reduces the opportunity to miss a paddle stroke.

Repair Kits

Whether you are on an inflatable or a solid board, you may need to undertake a temporary repair to the board. Most inflatables come with a repair kit consisting of adhesive and fabric. You never know when a problem might occur, so take these with you in your kit bag.

Garmin GPS and watch with heart rate monitor

There are various types of tape that can help to seal dings on solid boards. Keep these nearby to effect a quick repair and reduce the opportunity for water ingress into your board. If salt water gets into the core of a solid board, it can 'eat' away at the polystyrene and ruin it. If this occurs, the board will feel heavier than it used to.

Typical Garmin reports

CHAPTER 8

THE FLOW STATE, MASTERY & HAPPINESS

BEING IN FLOW

In 1990 Mihaly Csikszentmihalyi wrote a book called *Flow: The Psychology of Optimal Experience*. He set out to explain how humans get into the flow state. His work sparked a flurry of research into what makes people feel happy.

Csikszentmihalyi's studies concluded that happiness is an internal state of being attained through flow experiences.

Csikszentmihalyi described these characteristics of the flow state:

- Complete concentration on the task
- Clarity of goals and reward in mind and immediate feedback
- Transformation of time (speeding up / slowing down)
- The experience is intrinsically rewarding
- Feelings of effortlessness and ease
- There is a balance between challenge and skills
- Actions and awareness are merged, losing self-conscious rumination

Perhaps this is why SUP is so attractive and addictive. SUP often fulfils all the characteristics listed above.

Find yourself on a downwinder, linking the waves, constantly stepping backwards and forwards to trim the board with the wind at your back, and the chances are you will find flow. You won't be thinking about anything else but what you are doing. You will feel elation and a loss of the sense of time.

The same feelings can be accessed in whitewater, surfing waves or drafting.

Flow is not a permanent state, and its transience reflects the beauty of nature. The spell can be easily broken. But this reality only makes us value the elevated feelings more.

Flow stems from trust in ourselves and our capabilities. If you have any doubt or fear about what you are doing, you cannot find the flow state. Trusting in your own abilities is central to paddle mastery.

IN SEARCH OF PADDLE MASTERY

In his book *In the Flow*, Jonathan Males describes the four factors contributing to a paddler entering the feeling of mastery.

1. Motivation

Males suggests that motivation must be intrinsic (from inside you) rather than extrinsic (outside of you). If you are more motivated by winning than by putting in a good performance, then you will not achieve paddle mastery. People who race to win often drift away from paddling when they start to lose. It's worth reflecting on what motivates you.

Furthermore, any parent or coach should foster a performance mindset in their children not a mindset of winning. Apparently, the second-born tends to be more successful at sport than the first-born for this reason. The older sibling gets used to 'beating' their younger brother or sister as children. This sets up two different mindsets – one has an expectation of winning, and the other, an attitude of improving. The child who expects to win all the time finds it too hard to take when they lose.

2. Decision Making

Decision making determines the quality of performance. Good performers make the right decisions – be it recognising a route through rapids or a successful route on a downwinder. Mastery is about assimilating what is in front of you and making good decisions.

This relates to the learning cycle we looked at in Chapter 1. Decision making can only be improved by putting yourself in challenging situations, experiencing and reflecting on the results. As paddlers develop their skills and build confidence, they progress from conscious to unconscious competence. Good decisions become automatic.

3. Execution

Conscious thought is too slow to guide anyone through the dynamic demands of a paddle sport. Proper execution stems from practice and reinforcing greater trust in your abilities. Visualisation and mental rehearsal all assist in this regard. The more execution is 'unthought', the more you enter the flow state.

4. Teamwork

Paddling can be seen as an individual activity, but this is a short-sighted viewpoint. Teamwork is about concern and support for others. This is about building effective relationships with coaches, teammates and paddling buddies. This stems from being supportive and selfless to help others. Being part of a team (or community), sharing knowledge and providing feedback develops your identity as a paddler.

These 4 elements of paddle mastery form a valuable reference point for all paddlers.

Coming full circle and referring to Chapter 1, where we looked at goals and context, consider the following:

- Are my motivations in SUP sustainable?
- How will I continue to learn?
- How will I make my skills automatic?
- How can I support others to develop their skills and self-confidence?

CAN SUP IMPROVE MENTAL HEALTH?

In his book *Blue Mind*, Wallace Nichols studied the effect of water on people. His research concluded that when you see water, hear water, or even think about water, it triggers a response in your brain that immediately makes you feel calmer. He suggested that being in or on the water had these benefits:

Reduces stress: Being on, in or near water is proven to decrease the stress hormones in our body.

Increases ability to focus: Spending time near water helps you avoid burnout in our 'busy' lives. It increases your ability to focus and improves creativity.

Improve sleep: Spending time near, in or on water has been proven to help people with sleeping disorders. It reduces our stress levels and helps us feel relaxed, thus helping us sleep better at night. Even listening to water sounds before bed, like rainfall or ocean sounds, can induce a meditative state that brings on relaxation, helping lull the brain into falling asleep.

Reduce anxiety and depression disorders: Being near bodies of water can reduce symptoms of anxiety and depression. There are examples in his book of how SUP has helped with mental health disorders.

Allow you to connect with others: SUP takes away the technological distractions of modern life and allows you to focus your attention on the people you are with. It opens up the quality of conversation, strengthening relationships with others.

Our personal experience supports these findings and strengthens the addictive nature of SUP.

CONCLUDING THOUGHTS ON FLOW

SUP is far more complex than it first appears. It is the ultimate workout for the body and mind. It combines so many factors that fascinate humans. It is mentally and physically challenging and takes place in beautiful, natural environments. It is social and involves worthwhile activities such as continuous personal learning and supporting others. SUP is a route to finding flow (and therefore happiness), a feeling of personal mastery and long-lasting health.

We hope you continue to benefit from it as much as we do!

ACKNOWLEDGEMENTS

Andy and James would like to extend their thanks to many people who have helped directly or indirectly in writing this book. In no order they are:

Telmo Irigoyen: Coach and mentor at LeClercq Surfing
Machiel van Veen Levt: Clothing friend and supporter
Rachael Pereira: Photographer
Kinsa Dicks: SUP Yoga maestro
Guy Dinsdale: Whitewater fanatic
Barry Hughes: Whitewater guru
Tom Westaway: Whitewater fanatic
Glyn Smith: Whitewater fanatic
Dani Parres: SUP maestro
Albert Laborda: Photographer
LeClercq SUP team
Starboard
Nico Dinovo: UpSupping Magazine
Jane Burrows: Number 1 supporter
Jeremy Atkins: Fernhurst Books
Sophia Stephen: Sports Science Graduate

Photographs
All photographs © Rachael Pereira or Andy Burrows except:
Starboard: Front cover (bottom 2 circles); P24, P25 (right), 30 (top), 44 (middle), 52, 53, 63, 65 (left), 67, 70, 74 (top), 76, 77, 78, 79, 80, 108, 110 (left), 113, 116, 118, 131 (top right), 132 (bottom), 137, 149
Albert Laborda: Front cover (main image), P29 (top), 51, 109
Nico Dinovo: P71, P74 (bottom), P75, P110 (top right), 111, 115
Glyn Smith: P16 (left), 124, 126, 127
Guy Dinsdale: P106, 125 (right), 144 (bottom right)
Jeremy Atkins: P33 (top right)
Pixabay: Pexels: P33 (top left); 442683: P33 (middle); Keifit: P93 (left); Juuucy: P93 (right)
Shutterstock: Lilkin: Front cover (top circle); Xamyak: P40; Nicolas Primola: P46; Juan M. Portillo: P96 (left); txking: P110 (bottom right); GreyBerry: P120 (top)